Faith

Under Fire

Also by LaJoyce Brookshire

Soul Food
Web of Deception

Faith *Under* Fire

Betrayed by
a Thing Called *Love*

LaJoyce Brookshire

POCKET BOOKS
New York London Toronto Sydney

Pocket Books
A Division of Simon & Schuster, Inc.
1230 Avenue of the Americas
New York, NY 10020

Karen Hunter Publishing
A Division of Suitt-Hunter Enterprises, LLC
598 Broadway, 3rd Floor
New York, NY 10012

First Karen Hunter Publishing/Pocket Books hardcover edition
December 2007

POCKET and colophon are registered trademarks of
Simon & Schuster, Inc.

For information about special discounts for bulk purchases,
please contact Simon & Schuster Special Sales at
1-800-456-6798 or business@simonandschuster.com.

Designed by Mary Austin Speaker

Manufactured in the United States of America

10 9 8 7 6 5 4 3 2 1

ISBN-13: 978-1-4165-6645-8
ISBN-10:   1-4165-6645-7

But without faith it is impossible

to please Him: for he that cometh

to God must believe that He is, and

that He is a rewarder of them that

diligently seek Him.

— HEBREWS 11:6

For women everywhere who deeply love and trust their men. It is my prayer that you thoroughly examine the container and what it contains before leaping into love, by seeking the face of God through prayer.

In Memory of . . .

Fannie "Grannie" Hunter
Mary Celeste "Auntie" Hunter
Gus "Daddy" Brookshire, Sr.
Martha "Miss Lucille" Hubbard
Aunt Geraldine Turner
Aunt Marchita Jennings
George Howard
Barron Nathaniel Wright
The Notorious B.I.G.
Ruth Matthews
Rosa Lee Daniels
Mary Louise Daniels
Lenny Gordon
Rev. Cynthia "Ma" Vaughn
"Mama" Alma Robbins
Michael Ellis
Gregory "Dudy Bear" Wallis

Contents

Acknowledgments

I praise you, God, from whom all blessings flow, and I thank you for each and every one. I thank you, Lord, for giving me strength when I was weak and peace during the storm. You kept me safe and out of harm's way in order to complete the assignment that you have ordained, as this body of work has been orchestrated solely by you.

My dearest husband, Gus, and Bishop of the Brookshire household—I thank you for allowing me the room to share this story so that others may be set free. From the ages of twelve to seventeen you were a genius in gifting me with a diary annually. You could have bought me anything else with your Christmas money, but you chose a diary, and that was divine. It is ironic that the art of journalizing, inspired by you, would become a favorite pastime of mine and be utilized to share these accounts of my life with others. The conversations and turns of events that transpired during this time were accurately documented in my journals. Thank you for following your heart so that I may be able to share a piece of mine with the world—and I do mean a piece, because you have the rest! Who loves you, bay-bay?!

My sweet baby girl, Brooke Angel—thank you for not typing over Mommie's pages. Your very own computer is on the way.

My parents, Joana and Randy Baker—a.k.a. Jo & Bo—thank you for taking a break from all of that globetrotting to come see about your baby girl. I am eternally thankful that you had the means, the compassion, and the time to extend the love of Jesus in your hearts even when it was painful.

My dear brothers—thank you for not executing the threats, but thank you even more for your prayers. Stevie, your being here helped to remind me who we are, and whose we are.

Karen Hunter—from your days at the New York *Daily News* and my days at Arista Records, we've declared our sisterhood. You were among the first to believe in this story when no one else did, and you proved it with a feature on me in your column. Nothing gives me more pleasure than to be a scribe with your publishing company. I count it an honor and a privilege to have access to your vast intellectual capacity, which will undoubtedly inspire nations to read what you have deemed viable literature. Let's roll . . .

Many thank-yous are due to the valiant women and men of God through whose ministries my growth in the Lord has increased:

- My pastor, Rev. William Earl Lee, and his bride, Evangelist Verna Lee, for keeping the Word before the body of Jesus the Christ Church. And for walking in the Lord in all His ways, proving there will be no more—absolutely no more—bad days. Hallelujah!
- Bishop Sam Williams and family, for constantly keeping me lifted in prayer. As an adopted daughter, I hope I've made you proud.
- Rev. Henzy Green, Jr., for being a shining example of how to walk with Jesus right here on Earth.
- Apostle Clifford and Elect Lady Darlyn Turner, for depositing critical nuggets in my spirit that have elevated my walk with the Lord.

Thanks to the following ministries, which have come into my home via television and into my car via tapes, providing me with comfort and enlightenment during very dark times when I couldn't get to my own house of worship:

- Trinity Broadcasting Network, for being on twenty-four hours a day!
- Bishop Noel Jones, for awakening my intellection in Jesus.
- Bishop T. D. Jakes, I know I'm a woman loose.
- Pastor Rod Parsley, for teaching me how to give up my this, for that!
- Bishop Eddie Long, for teaching me how to stand during the in-between.
- Bishop Ulmer, I can now say, "Forward march!"

- Pastor Creflo Dollar, I've learned the importance of tithing.
- Prophetess Juanita Bynum, I now live Rapture Ready!
- Bishop Clarence McClendon, I know now that the field *is* the world and not just arrangements, decorations, and props.

To my team of caregivers—I need another book to write about how much I appreciate you: Stacey and Claudette Dyches, Mayla Billips, Theresa Gibbs, Rev. Kenneth Pearman, Skip and Diane Anderson, Larry and Patsy Parkins and family, Uncle Charles and Aunt Peggy and family, Ruth Matthews, and Nurse Tracey Sheptuk. A special thanks to Zee Dees and the Webster family, who specifically cared for me.☺

To my Morning Commanders on the Fourth Watch Prayer Line—the world can reap the benefit of what God has done in us and through us, *and* manifested, because of our faithfulness at 5 A.M. every day. We indeed are fitly joined together. You have all been a blessing in my life. Though most of us have never met and probably never will, we know one another in the Spirit. I look forward to our continued reports of praise and our growth as we stay on the Wall. Apostles Kim and Ardell Daniels, thank you for your obedience in coordinating such a mighty network of Commanders to capture each morning.

To my Armor Bearers: Evangelist Linda McBride, Ellie Winslow, Andrea Francis, Evan Mykol Blake, Deaconess Bonita White, and Aracely Mitchell. I am indebted to you for taking the call of coverage seriously. I continue to pray for your strength in the Lord as you keep me in prayer. Claudette Dyches (my first Armor Bearer), although you are not physically able to travel anymore, your prayers are always received when I step onto the field of the world.

To my team—thanks for miraculously keeping all of the balls in the air: attorney Pamela Crockett Fish (aaaah, the power of an anointed attorney!); marketing mavens Michelle Joyce Johnson, Kalima Lewis, and Stacey Murray; scriptwriting partner Blake Roberts; producer Irving Wright; and photographer Elijah Muhammad.

To my friends who have loved me through the good and bad days—I've been able to count on your prayers when it mattered most, and that's what friends and family are for: Mama Brookshire, Susan Ellis, Theresa Gibbs, Faye Harrington Davis, Angela Henderson, Debbie Bryant, Lencola Sullivan-Verseveldt, Mona Lynn Wallis, Walter Briggs, E. Lynn Harris, Larry and Debra Esposito, Steve and Terri Ewing, Jimmy and Nanette Nelson, LeNardo and Olivia Nelson, Karu Daniels, Shontisha Huntley, Mike Hill, Lonai Mosley, Darwyn and Velma Ingrahm, Gordette "Sloopy" Brent, Pamela Avery, Dewanda Howard, Eric Dove, Kaye Cooksey, Ron and Indira Singh, Eric Dove, Dr. Cynthia Howell, Terria Ladner, Johnetta Boone,

Theara Ward, Joanne Branham (a.k.a. Marcenda Ry), Arlene McGruder, Maria Davis, Renee Foster, Tri Smith, LT Ladino, and big and little "Star" Olga and Zuli Turner.

To my National Black Leadership Commission on AIDS family—how awesome to be in the house at the time I needed you most. Nobody but God orchestrated such an assignment. Debra Fraser-Howze: I am your little sister, and our lives are forever sealed as together we have experienced the death of Barron. Never has such a sad day penetrated my soul so deeply as that rainy April afternoon. Consider me always available to you as you march in the struggle.

Johnny Allen, Bugsy, and Vaughn Harper—I know that you too were caught in the deception. No hard feelings, I still love you.

To all of my author friends who have paved the way, sharing publishing horrors for me to avoid, teaching me how to tour, praising me when I did well, and lovingly correcting me when I did wrong—I love you and appreciate you now and always: Lolita Files (my Libra Twin), Victoria Christopher Murray, Eric Jerome Dickey, E. Lynn Harris, Brenda Stone Browder, Benilde Little, and Zane.

To Brooke Angel's caregivers—when I'm on the road or keeping late nights, thank you for being in our village to help raise my baby: Marion Blount, Mayla Billips, Dr. Cynthia Howell, and Kathy Williams.

To all my Mamas on my block, down the street, and around the corner in Chicago—thanks for helping to raise me.

It is my hope that I continue to be a beacon of light for the Lord.

In His Service . . . LaJoyce

Foreword

Brenda Stone Browder
Author, _On the Up and Up: A Survival Guide for
Women Living with Men on the Down Low_

God has given me the opportunity to reach scores of women, connecting with their spirits to bring understanding to the "down low" phenomenon. I am amazed at the number of women who have found themselves in the same types of relationships that I had. For years, I truly felt as if this was only my plight, as if I was the only one whose husband cheated with men. This journey has enlightened me. This journey has broadened the scope of my vision of this unbelievable reality.

On the Up and Up has actually enhanced my life. A friend told me to get ready for the second half of my life to be totally different from the first. I am fifty years old, and given that people do live to be a hundred, I am starting the second half of my life right now. From the beginning of my fiftieth year, things have not been the same. My relationship with Christ has deepened. I attribute this to my deliverance from all that was suffocating my growth. All of that hurt, pain, and guilt from my past has been erased.

LaJoyce, like me and the growing numbers of women who refuse to stand by silently allowing the stigmas and dangers of HIV/AIDS to continue, is sharing her story to take back the control and take back the power that HIV/AIDS has stolen from lives, relationships, and families.

Like Shadrach, Meshach, and Abednego, she stood firm in her faith and came out of the fire victorious.

When LaJoyce discovered she had been lied to, selfishly, and that her life had been purposely placed in jeopardy, she was ready to put one hand on her hip and the other on the door handle to throw the relationship out with the trash. But instead, she remembered her faith and chose not to take on the persona of a mad black woman. LaJoyce chose to take the higher ground and stand firm in her faith. She stood by her husband until God called him home. LaJoyce stayed the course and ran the race and is now able to soar like an eagle, overcoming the tests of being in an uneven relationship. She understands that it is not about her, but about others who lack the deep roots of her faith.

God places people together on purpose for a purpose, and it is no different with LaJoyce and I. The message remains on my voice mail today from her "play-brother" Walter Briggs. It was in 2003, and he was trying to make arrangements for us to get together. He and I met coincidentally at a local festival in Ohio because he didn't want to wait in a long line to buy a pie. As I passed him my writer's card, he told me I should speak with his sister, LaJoyce, who novelized *Soul Food*.

Initially, LaJoyce and I were to speak just as writer to writer, but when I saw her on my ex-husband J. L. King's video *No More Secrets, No More Lies*, discussing her deceased husband, I knew we had to get together. Finally, it was Karen Hunter who put us together and sealed our relationship, and now we continue this work of sharing our truths in the vineyard.

For LaJoyce to expose her life with a man who tried until his dying day to keep his fight against AIDS a secret (as so many sadly do) because of the stigma that is attached to the disease is an act of heroism. She is willing to stand out before all—bearing her life, accepting both kudos and criticisms—and continue with divine guidance to slay the stigmas.

This great literary work, *Faith Under Fire: Betrayed by a Thing Called Love*, will serve those who have the privilege of reading it. Those who have had similar experiences will find solace in knowing that they are not alone. Those who have not will gain valuable information for self-empowerment. And those who are apathetic will gain understanding that turning their backs will not immunize them from HIV/AIDS touching their lives.

If not for the grace of God, there go I. . . .

Introduction

Debra Fraser-Howze
President/CEO,
National Black Leadership Commission on AIDS

This book is the story of one African-American woman, but it is really the story or potential story of us all. One in every fifty African-American men and one in every hundred and sixty African-American women is estimated to be infected with HIV, the virus that causes AIDS, in America, according to the U.S. Centers for Disease Control (2006). We are a community in the midst of a public health emergency, and like the victims of Katrina, we are out there all on our own.

There are some things in the history of black people that we should never allow to be repeated—the obvious one is slavery, and another is HIV/AIDS. But there are many, many more.

In my years of service to my community and country, I have been a presidential appointee to both the Clinton and George W. Bush administrations, developed my own agency to help black leaders respond to HIV/AIDS, raised millions in new funding for prevention, conducted research, developed legislation, and fought for education and prevention programs at all levels and in all communities of color. Our organization was the first to involve the black church and leadership in a formal action plan in response to this epidemic, and we have conducted public policy and communality development since 1987. We have a very long way to go, and HIV/AIDS is not the last fatal disease with no cure that our community will face in the next few years.

And we are far from prepared.

But as the history of this disease is written, let it not discount the black people who unknowingly faced imminent danger because they loved another, or those who lived in perpetual fear of this disease, or those who took the responsibility to get tested and know their status and protected themselves from a preventable infection to save both themselves, their lovers, and the loved ones around them from the devastation that this disease causes.

A friend of mine repeated a saying that has stuck with me for my entire life. She said that one day we will all get to Heaven, and before we meet our maker, we as black people will first meet our ancestors and be made to respond to one question: "What did you do with your freedom?"

Based on your answer it will be determined if you used your freedom to advance the cause of your people and lived your life in a way that helped others. It is a profound commentary and a question we should all live our lives preparing to answer. We all have free will. It takes a great deal of personal responsibility to live a life that answers this question well and betters your family, your community, your people, and yourself.

It is believed in some circles that we all come here knowing how we are going to leave and that we make this decision before we are sent. In this book, several people made decisions, all of which they will be required to answer for. Make your decision the right one.

LaJoyce, a beautiful, talented woman, made a decision to honor her marriage vows and care for a dying husband. Throughout this journey, information about the way he acquired his HIV infection and how long he knew about it would have reshaped the thinking of any normal human being. But LaJoyce was not just any woman; she was a woman of great faith. Through this one journey in her life, which God allowed me to be a part of from its beginning, I learned much about the power of love and the unimaginable power of faith. Faith in things unseen and unknown will pull you through in times when you are most in need.

What the African-American community must grapple with as we read LaJoyce's story is how we got here in the first place. While conspiracy theories abound in our community—from the evil white scientist, to the government, to man-made agents that all went awry and purposely caused the untimely death of millions of African descendants, leaving behind forty million orphans—these theories are just one part of the possible story.

When the history of HIV/AIDS in communities of

African descent is written, it will be full of stories like the one LaJoyce is telling, including our collective responsibility to halt a preventable disease that kills and for which there is still no cure.

What have you done with your freedom?

If your answer is that you did not take precautions to save your own life as a woman of African descent, or if it's that you were a black man on the "down low" or having unprotected sex and you knew there was a big disease with a little name that was sexually transmitted and took no precautions to protect your mate, then your answer to the question is catastrophic.

The answer to how and why we got here in this thing called AIDS lies at the feet of many. The black community are a people who have thrown caution to the wind, in a society that is so racially divided that it would cut off from black people resources that flowed in the first wave of a supposedly white epidemic when they thought they had found progress for their own; we are an advocacy community that held each other close when it was convenient and all but abandoned each other when it was not; we have a government so crippled with disdain for some of its citizens that it was easily blinded into abandoning them and leaving them to deal with a life-threatening situation—and never really told us in the beginning that we were already infected and that this would be our destruction; we are a people who went along with laws that were not in the best interest of our communities' health; we are black men and women who do not think themselves worthy to stay alive;

and, as this book points out, we have a group of brothers, not all but some, who are simply doing the wrong thing and putting sisters at great risk.

We can fix this! Black women can fix anything!

We can get the individual information we need by getting tested and protect all those that we love. We can stop second-guessing our questions about some men and deal with their real sexual issues. We can do a little more due diligence before we choose a lifelong mate who will help us bear our children. We can say "You have to use a condom," no matter what our age or the environment we come from, and change our attitude about ourselves so we know we are worth protecting.

And if all else fails, we can do what we do with our children and simply take a "time out" until we get all the information that will keep us safe. We are not a bankrupt community and we deserve to be safe; if he says no to a condom, we are worthy enough to say good-bye.

Sistahs, you are descendants of kings and queens. Do not let our present condition confuse you out of your royal position. Love black men like there are no other men on the face of the earth, but never allow any one of them to remove the blessing from the bosom of our people.

Take care of yourselves. LaJoyce did with body and soul. And she continues to bless us with all that she is and all the potential she has realized. Walk good and walk safe, and remember: You are all potential queens of the dynasty that is still to come in black America.

CHAPTER ONE

The Meeting

But seek ye first the kingdom of God, and his righteousness;
and all these things shall be added unto you.

— MATTHEW 6:33

I t happened quite suddenly, my falling in love. You know the kind I'm talking about—that *bam*, love-at-first-sight kind of love.

It was January 30, 1990. I was a part-time speech teacher at the Queens Broadcasting Center, in the Jamaica section of Queens, New York. My full-time job was as writer/producer of entertainment and information programming at the Sheridan Broadcasting Network at One Times Square Plaza in New York City.

The day before, I had decided to take a "sick" day. I cleaned off my desk, returned all phone calls, and handed in the weekly scripts a day early—much to the delight of my executive producer.

On my "sick" day, I took a lengthy bubble bath, washed my hair, and lazed around until it was time to get to class.

For some reason, I dressed carefully, in a red silk blouse, leather pants, and high-heeled pumps. It was quite snazzy attire for a teacher who was about to spend the next four hours correcting speech patterns for on-air hopefuls.

About an hour into my class, I excused myself to make copies of handouts. On my way to the copy machine, I glanced into the recording studio and saw the tallest, finest honey-dipped colored man I had ever laid eyes on in my life. I ran to the office of the director, longtime on-air personality Johnny Allen, of New York City's KISS-FM, to inquire about the eye candy I had just glimpsed.

Johnny replied, "Oh, that's Steven. He's a really nice guy."

"Hmm, Steven," I said. "I have a brother named Stephen; what a coincidence."

While at the copier, I took another long look at the honey-dip, giving him points on his name alone, before returning to my class.

When we were saying good-byes for the evening, Johnny introduced me to Steven and I turned as red as my blouse, overwhelmed by his charming demeanor. Johnny announced that he had arranged for Steven to take me home.

"Take me home? All the way to *Brooklyn*?" I asked.

We were in Queens—a forty-five-minute train ride and easily an hour-plus drive away.

"I'll take you all the way to Pennsylvania, if that's where you live," Steven said.

I raised an "is this guy for real" eyebrow at Johnny, and he winked a sign of approval.

"Let's roll," I said, gathering my things.

On the ride home, Steven and I exchanged regular pleasantries, asked typical questions, and laughed a lot. He kept thanking God. I liked that part. Since I come from a Baptist-born-and-bred background, God is indeed at the top of my list.

"Why do you keep saying 'Thank you, God'?" I asked.

"I wasn't even supposed to be at the school tonight," he said. "I missed my final because I was in the hospital and I had to complete it tonight. So I'm saying 'Thank you, God' because I wouldn't have met you if I hadn't been in the hospital."

The reporter in me was piqued. "Why were you in the hospital?"

"Bleeding ulcers."

"Bleeding ulcers!?" I asked in disbelief, contorting my face. "How old are you?"

"Thirty-one," he answered. "I've just had a lot of problems—a bad marriage and lots of stress in my job. But now that I've met you, all of that is about to change."

We continued with pleasant conversation and before we knew it we looked up and had no idea where we were. We were lost somewhere between Queens and Brooklyn. The only way he knew how to get us out of the circle we seemed to be driving in was to go all the way to Manhattan and then to Brooklyn. Our one-hour ride turned into three hours.

We finally arrived at my front door, where we exchanged numbers. He waited at his car to see that I had made it safely into my apartment. I looked out of the window to wave and he was still there, leaning against his car, looking up at my window. He acknowledged my wave with a beep of his car horn. As much as I hated to admit it, I was soaring from my evening with Steven.

The next day at work in the studio, we had WBLS-FM on in the background while making preparations for our weekly syndicated production. All of a sudden, we heard deejay Bugsy announce, "Here is 'Ready or Not' by After 7 for LaJoyce Hunter from Steven. He wants her to know that he's coming for her—ready or not!"

My office mates and I screamed. And my phone started ringing off the hook. Everyone wanted to know who this *Steven* was. My reply was the same: "Some dude I met yesterday!"

Being in the radio and record business had some advantages, and one of them was access to the hotline number for the deejay booth at WBLS. The other was knowing Bugsy personally. After fielding phone calls from friends, I called Bugsy myself to inquire about how in the world this Steven managed to get him to make such a declaration before *and* after "Ready or Not" played.

"I know Steven, too," Bugsy told me. "He is a part-time producer with Vaughn Harper's *Quiet Storm* syndicated radio program for Japan."

Vaughn Harper was the premier nighttime voice in New York and was like a father to me in the business. Bugsy and I had always been really friendly with one another and he was like a big brother.

He issued his stamp of approval: "Now Steven is someone I'd *really* like to see you with. I can vouch for him all the way."

"Really?" I said, knowing that Bugsy had shared his disdain for the last guy from the station I had dated.

"Yep. Really," he said, mindful of that previous situation.

"Thanks, Bugs," I said. "I'll keep you posted."

Later that afternoon, a deliveryman brought two dozen red, long-stemmed American Beauties from Steven. This guy was really pouring it on and I loved it!

I phoned to thank him for the roses and the dedication, and he invited me to dinner the following evening. We went to a very pricey restaurant on the East River and we both had lobster and champagne. He had another dozen roses at the restaurant for me.

"These are for you to keep at home," he said, as the others were for me to keep at my office.

At least twice a week from then on, Steven romanced me with dinners at expensive restaurants. And between the dinners, we were always going to some event. As a producer of entertainment programming, I always had tickets to concerts, plays, or new movies in town. My responsibilities kept me out at least three nights a week. We always got two complimentary tickets to an event, so Steven became my new "hot date."

The dinners became his way of controlling some of our outings since it was a given that we would attend a promotional event. We ended up going out five nights a week!

For the first three months of our dating, Steven had

roses delivered to my job every week until I told him to stop. It was established early on that we were both definitely in love. Like I said, it was love at first sight.

It was signed, sealed, and delivered by the time we had sex, intensifying the blush of our new love.

Steven further locked in the relationship by introducing me to his mother and two sisters. They all lived in the family home in Lakeview, New York, a predominantly black middle-class Long Island town. We all got along extremely well, and his older sister and I could pass for sisters. We both have that *café con leche* (with lots of *leche*) skin, light-brown-eyes-and-sandy-hair thing going on. When we went out together people always asked us if we were sisters, and we'd just laugh and say, "Yes!"

We did a lot of flaunting one another in front of our friends. It was mutual that there was nothing but love between us all. Steven's best friend, Stacey, and his wife, Claudette, were the best of our buddies. They were one crazy pair. We'd go to midnight bowling almost every weekend and win all of the trivia games, like guessing musical artists. *Yeah, right!* I'd only eaten and slept music for the last I-don't-know-how-many years. I was a shoo-in.

We discussed many times if it was even fair for me to play because I was in the entertainment business, but we'd just shrug and collect our prizes. The real superstar of that game was Claudette. We dubbed that girl "the foremost knowledgeable person about information that don't mean s-h-i-t." She needs to be a contestant on pop culture trivia shows; I guarantee you, she would win. To this day, Claudette and Stacey are permanent fixtures in my life.

Steven and I were spending so much time together every night that he had a hard time getting himself to his job at Bayside BMW, where he was the assistant parts manager. He had practically moved into my Brooklyn apartment, too. But I refused to say that he "lived" there. That was against my religion. I wasn't playing house with anyone. Plus, my mother would have killed me!

It was easier for him to bring a bag with his stuff in it every week for whatever we would be attending and leave for work from there. He definitely tried to move in on me, though, putting stuff in my closet. But I would take his clothes out of the closet that he'd leave hanging there and pack them for him every day, and I refused to give him space in my drawer.

Call me old fashioned, but it was bad enough that I was sleeping with this dude and he wasn't my husband. I knew better.

At the time, I had a male roommate named Derrick. Now, *his* girlfriend Tina did live with us. They met at Columbia University. Derrick was an awesome budding attorney at one of the top law firms in midtown Manhattan, and Tina was an accountant. We needed to share the apartment because neither of us could afford the rent alone for the magnificent two-bedroom, two-bathroom apartment in Brooklyn's Clinton Hill section. Our rent was twelve hundred dollars a month in 1989! Steven offered to help pay my portion of the rent, but I flatly refused.

By December 1, 1990—just eleven months after our first meeting—we were married. The ride to the altar was rocky, as was all that followed the wedding. Here is my real-life tale—the tale of a woman betrayed by a thing called love, a tale of putting my faith under fire.

Read on and learn. . . .

CHAPTER TWO

The Wedding

He who findeth a wife findeth a good thing . . .

—PROVERBS 18:22

One Sunday evening in June 1990, at Steven's home, we were having champagne in his sister's room, watching movies. When I got to the bottom of my glass, I almost swallowed a diamond ring! The whole family knew about his plan and when I screamed, everyone came into the room to offer congratulations.

We got out the calendar and immediately began looking for the best dates to get married. At his mother's insistence, we chose December 1. It was less than six months away! We had work to do—a lot of work. My hometown is Chicago and a girl just *has* to get married in her hometown—at least that's what Emily Post says.

In my opinion, the first thing we needed to do was to get ourselves a budget and stick to it. When we started analyzing our finances, I discovered that Steven was $30,000 in debt!

"Steven, you've got to stop using your credit cards now, or we'll never get married," I told him. "How did you get this much in debt?"

"Well, I put new windows on the house for my mother," he said. "You know I like to wear nice clothes. Our dinners, the roses . . ."

My head was spinning. All of those dinners and roses and nice clothes contributed to this mass of debt? Yes, he did love to dress well and he shopped in places like Saks Fifth Avenue, Macy's, Nordstrom, and small boutiques. He had recently bought a line of new outfits so that he could hang out with me, he said. I saw that one price tag was $550 for a matching sweater, turtleneck, and pants outfit.

"You're done," I told him. "No more roses, no more dinners, no more five-hundred-dollar outfits. You're done! From this day forward, you're on a budget. I don't want to get married and be under all of this debt. Maybe we should wait to get married until you can clear up most of it."

His mother heard me say this to him and interjected that she would help him pay down his debt.

"It's hard to find true love," she said. "Don't let money stop you from getting married. Most people would never get married if they waited until they had the money. I'll help him. Will your parents help you with your debt?"

"My debt?" I asked, as I showed her the worksheet I'd created. "I only have six hundred and fifty dollars' worth of rent and utilities. My Grannie taught me to use cash. And while I like to shop, I have never spent five hundred and fifty dollars on any one outfit and I doubt if I ever will."

When I met Steven, I was planning to leave New York

by year's end. I believed the cliché "If you make it in New York, you can make it anywhere." My goal was to work for six years in New York City, save my money, go back to Chicago, buy a four-to-six-family rental unit, move back into my room at Mommie's house, and become a real estate mogul in addition to writing entertainment shows.

The differences in our financial views on the day of our engagement were very clear. Instead of us celebrating, we spent the rest of the evening writing budgets with his mother until it was time for her to get to her nursing job at Mercy Hospital.

She left us that evening with one thought I'll never forget: "There's nothing wrong with buying nice clothes and having nice things, LaJoyce. Steven is accustomed to really nice things."

I thought out loud, "Yeah, but at whose expense? Now that Steven is going to get married, his spending habits need to change."

The South Side of Chicago versus the Long Island upbringing conflicts were in full swing!

Steven's mother insisted that I call her Mom. Her name was Mozelle, so I dubbed her Mama Mo. My mother's name is Joana and many of her friends call her Jo, and my stepfather's name is Bo. So we had Mo, Jo, and Bo.

I gave Steven a card one evening to express what I was feeling at the time:

You've found the key to my happiness without my having to tell you. You've found the key to my laughter without my

having to tell you. You've found the key to my love without
my having to tell you. The key that I do want to give to you is
the one to my house.

Then I handed him a key to my apartment. He was
speechless! He was always there after he had carte blanche
to come over. He had practically moved in then, because
now he had a key.

My girlfriend from high school, Kaye, who was a flight
attendant based out of LaGuardia Airport for six months,
used to stay over. But she was forced to sleep in the window seat because Steven was constantly there. I felt guilty,
but she insisted she didn't mind.

The one thing that we had to do immediately was go to
Chicago so that he could meet my family and see where
and how I was raised. I had already called several hotels
and made appointments for us to check out a few venues
where the wedding might take place that December.

We drove to Chicago in July, and upon our arrival at
four in the morning, Steven wanted to check into a local
motel and sleep before going to my house. I flatly refused,
because my father knew what time we left and would be
worried if we didn't show up at the appointed hour. The
motel he wanted to check into was a flea-bitten one on
Stony Island Avenue!

"You don't roll into Chicago, honey, and check into the
wrong motel at four A.M. when a girl's father is waiting for
her to show up," I told him. "You do New York and your
people, let *me* navigate Chicago."

"But, I want to snuggle with you tonight," he cried. "I'm not going to be able to sleep in the same bed with you the whole time we're here."

"You got that right!" I said. "But you'll survive. We're here for you to meet my parents and my friends, and to find a place for a wedding. You can get your butt rubbed back at home. You will have to wait."

This conversation spun out of control into our first huge argument. He ranted like a three-year-old who couldn't get his way.

"But I'm tired," he whined. "I need a shower. I want to be fresh when I meet your mother. I'm cranky. I'm horny. And I want to sleep until I'm ready to wake up."

I wasn't listening to him. I got tired of arguing with him, so I just kept quiet and simply drove up in front of my parents' house and got out of the car. My father opened the door and said, "Right on time!"

I threw Steven a knowing look that said "See?"

At 9 A.M. my best friend in the whole wide world, Theresa, whom I lovingly call Tyger, bounded into the house full of energy to scoop me up so I could go out with her to talk. But first, she went to the guest room to check out the sleeping fiancé. I thought she was just going to peek at him, but when she flipped on the light to get a good look he woke up. I heard them speaking but I didn't know what they were discussing.

It wasn't until years later that Tyger told me he cussed her out. I was floored. She knew better than to tell me that crap then, because he would have been an ex-fiancé before he even got the chance to say good morning to my mama. Knowing me the way a best-friend-in-the-whole-wide-world should know you, she decided not to tell me.

This is also why I brought him home. I needed to know if Steven could play well with others. My "significant others" who preceded him had all had to take this test. If I brought someone home for the "Crest Test" and they passed, we were good to go. But if they failed . . . Cussing out my best friend is certainly an "F." If I had only known.

We left him sleeping and I returned two hours later to find him getting dressed to meet the folks. He was laboring over what to wear.

"Put on your sweats," I said. "It's my mama, not some industry party."

"Are you kidding?" he said. "I'm meeting your *mother* for the first time; I have to come correct."

"Believe me, she won't be judging your outfit," I said. "Hurry up! Breakfast is on the stove."

When he came down, he was decked out in a three-piece matching outfit with gold jewelry on his neck, wrists, and fingers. At eleven in the morning he looked like he was ready for an evening out. My mama was still in her robe, and as I had speculated, my parents never said a word about what he was wearing. Steven charmed them as only he could, and my parents were hooked.

Due to the less-than-six-months-away wedding date, all of the hotels in town kept referring me to the Guest Quarter Suites Hotel on North Michigan Avenue, which was under construction. Mommie, Steven, and I went downtown for a tour. When the catering director handed us hard hats, we were surprised. Only the first two floors and the top two floors were completed. The ballroom, in which we were to have our wedding, was not completely finished either. The good thing was, since we were standing in an incomplete hotel wearing a hard hat and had no real samples of what the room would look and feel like, not to mention no food to taste, the price of the wedding for two hundred and fifty people was quite reasonable. My mother's face lit up like a Christmas tree.

During the rest of our visit, friends and family flooded the house to meet the husband-to-be. He was showered with hugs, warm welcomes, and lots of hushed corner conversations. It seemed as if Steven was passing the Crest Test from my people, and I was very happy.

One friend from Indianapolis, Henzy, told me when we hugged that he sensed another presence around me and that Steven and I must be very close. Henzy and I had been longtime friends, business partners, and spiritual prayer warriors since the mid-1980s. I valued and trusted his spiritual discernment and wisdom.

In Long Island, Steven was in the habit of driving me around to neighborhoods and showing me the girls' houses where he had "gotten the panties." It was an awesome conquest for him to have run through entire neighborhoods, and he was proud of it.

While in Chicago he asked me, "Where are some of your old boyfriends' houses?"

"I've only had two boyfriends here," I told him. "But I'll drive you by Gus's house first."

Why he wanted to see an old boyfriend's home, I'll never know. I drove up in front of the house.

"There it is!" I announced.

Steven knew the whole story with me and Gus Brookshire. We were boyfriend and girlfriend from the age of twelve to seventeen, with several breakups along the way. Gus was definitely my first true love. We'd promised ourselves that we'd get married sometime after college, when we'd had a chance to experience life. Gus joined the Air Force and moved to Texas, and I moved to New York. In 1989, Gus called me one night to announce his engagement. I cried my eyes out and wrote him a tear-stained letter, but told myself it was time to find myself a husband, too. One year later, there I was with my fiancé in front of Gus's house. *Nah, nah, nah, nah-nah!*

As Steven was admiring the flowers in Gus's yard, we heard a knock-knock on the hood of the car. There was Gus! I threw the car into park, and Gus grabbed me out and swung me around in the street. We stood there hugging and screaming in our surreal moment.

Mama Brookshire, Gus's mother, came to Steven's rescue with a hug.

"I'm Mama," she said. "Oh, you must be Steven. Well, we've heard so much about you. Just park the car, honey. That's her brother; don't mind them. You come on inside."

He did as he was told while Gus and I bounded into the house, arm in arm. We visited for about an hour and then excused ourselves, because we were on a tight schedule. In the car Steven stated, "I don't know why you didn't get married to Gus."

"He married someone else and that's all there was to it."

"But you've got to ask *your*self, why?"

The way he said it was such a failed attempt to dig at my self-esteem that I drove the car around the block and back in front of Gus's house.

"Get out of the car, *you* ask him!" I said.

He started stuttering.

"Yeah, that's what I thought," I said. "Aren't you glad he didn't marry me so you could?"

"Yes, I am," he admitted, and kissed me to seal the deal and apologize.

Back in New York, I had an August weekend fete for my bridesmaids to meet the designer I had chosen, Franklin Rowe, so he could create their gowns for the wedding. My mother flew in for the occasion and to meet Mama Mo. Franklin was the most awesome designer of the day and I had several knockout pieces from him. For our December wedding, the color scheme was emerald green and ivory velvet. I was wearing an ivory beaded bodice with an ivory velvet skirt. The whole idea was to have this gorgeous beaded top to wear later with ivory pants, and a slimming skirt in velvet and satin.

Mo and Jo hit it off immediately. Upon their first introduction, they were giggling like little kids as they jumped in the car and headed to the mall in search of the perfect color for them both. They decided to wear the same color and the same material but different-style dresses. Mo and Jo were gone for so long we started to worry.

When they returned, well after dark, I told Steven, "Well, they could have come back in an hour saying, 'I can't stand that woman.' Shopping together for a full eight hours means they love each other."

Steven was wearing an ivory brocade blazer with velvet pants. Being the fashionista he was, he wanted to have a second blazer made to change into at the reception, half brocade and half velvet. I had to admit that it was incredibly sharp. His garments were going to cost more than mine. I reminded him that he was over our wedding budget *and* his personal budget by getting two jackets.

"It's our wedding, don't you want me to be sharp?" he whined.

"Yeah," I said, but thinking, *He can't give Franklin a credit card*. My additional items to go with my gown weren't going to be made until after the wedding, and not until I needed them and could afford them. Like I mentioned, I had several Franklin Rowe originals, and they weren't cheap. I'd known Franklin about six years and I bought one item annually. At that very moment, cheap is what I was accused of being.

I wanted the girls to be in emerald-green velvet suits with rhinestone buttons. But each of the girls' dresses would be different to reflect their personalities. I was a victim of the "closet full of ugly bridesmaid's dresses" syndrome and I vowed it would end with me. I wanted their dresses to be a take-away item to wear again and again.

My mother; my girls, Pam, Lencola, Tyger, and Mayla; Mama Mo; and Steven's two sisters crowded into my apartment for an afternoon with Franklin. He sat back and watched us engage with one another for hours, and one by one he called the girls over to him. He was sketching each girl based on what he had observed. All of them let out a squeal of delight at what he had done and he proceeded to take their measurements. The designs were awesome. No one was disappointed.

Fuchsia was the color of choice for the moms, and satin was the material. Both of them stood at five feet two, and Franklin came up with exquisite designs.

The designs were under way, the hotel was selected, and I was getting married.

Weeeeee dawgie! We were gonna have a wedding!

It was time for me to renew the lease on my apartment, but Steven and his mother came up with the bright idea of having me move into a room in their house to save money for our new apartment until the wedding. I protested at first because the extra room was currently for family storage. We made a big party out of cleaning it out, and it took every bit of an entire weekend for it to be cleaned and organized.

When I moved in, Mama Mo had one rule: Steven was not allowed to sleep in my room. I agreed that would be the proper thing to do. Steven protested to the point of a full argument with his mom. I was shocked that he didn't see such an act as disrespectful in his mother's home. The other rules were general good roommate considerations: Clean up behind yourself, don't hog the bathroom, take a message if someone calls. . . .

I was easy in the kitchen department since I didn't eat the kinds of foods they ate. They were one carnivorous family! I didn't and still don't eat red meat. Instead I eat lots of raw foods, fruits, and nuts. They dubbed me "Rabbit," and I don't know who started it first, but Steven called me that all of the time. I always told them that eating right, going to bed early, taking dance classes, and taking long walks would keep me looking young forever. They could make fun of my garbage salads, complete with red cabbage (yum), and my 9 P.M. bedtime all they wanted.

PolyGram Records had a Las Vegas Night for one of their artists, and it was set up just like a real casino. They issued tickets for various prizes, and the grand prize was a trip to the Bahamas. Steven was a big winner, earning lots of tickets and, of course, jockeying for the Bahamas trip. Everyone there rallied around us. Several of my industry friends collected tickets from others so that we would have the most.

"Give them your tickets," they shouted. "They're getting married!"

Sure enough, we won the Bahamas trip. Everyone there was very happy for us. It was like having an unofficial engagement party.

We took the Bahamian trip over Labor Day weekend. Steven was angry about the accommodations, which consisted of a basic Howard Johnson–type room—two steps up from a dive. He wanted to check out and go to a luxury resort. I was not in the mood to have an argument, but I had to continue to be sagacious for the sake of our financial future.

"All we have to do is sleep in here, Steven," I said. "Let's just go and enjoy the beaches and the rest of the island. Can't you stay focused? This trip didn't cost us a dime."

"We *do* have to pay for food," he said.

"And because you like to eat in five-star restaurants, that will cost us more than this trip cost PolyGram," I said. "Let's have some good meals, reasonably priced, some good beach time, and stay right here. It's only four days."

He reluctantly did stay, but not without constant reminders of his dissatisfaction every time we came into the room. He would pout himself to sleep. I wasn't feeling too well, and I chalked it up to the rush-rush of the trip, the wedding planning, and the move. It was on this trip that I learned to pay Steven no mind at all. My biological father, Duke, taught me one very valuable lesson: "Don't try to be logical with illogical people."

When we got back home I made the most awesome discovery: I was pregnant! At twenty-eight, here I was getting married to my dream man and about to have a baby. I'd be only five months pregnant walking down the aisle, and that would be fine with me. So Henzy *was* right; the other presence he sensed around me was a baby!

Steven had quite a different reaction. He wanted us to keep it hush-hush. He said it wasn't a good idea to tell people you were pregnant before three months. I had heard that somewhere, too. So I agreed. I told no one.

One week later, he told me that he wasn't ready to start a family right away and that he wanted me to have an abortion so that we could start out right. He lamented about the relationship with his first wife, who already had a toddler when they got married, and said it was very hard for them to get established with a "crumb snatcher" in tow.

I told him he was nuts. Just like his mother said we should not wait on money to get married, I thought we should not toss out the baby because of money. We'd make it if he wanted to make it.

"Think about it very carefully," I suggested as I bounced off to take my evening walk.

The next Saturday morning, Steven woke me up at 6 A.M., fully dressed in a suit. "Get dressed," he said.

I didn't know where we were going, so I put on a dress, stockings, and pumps. We drove deeper into Long Island and he pulled up to a nondescript office building.

When we got inside I could clearly see this was a doctor's office. He gave my name at the window and they handed him some papers, which he gave to me, saying, "I've thought about it. I don't want to start off with a baby."

Whaaaaaat! I screamed in my head. That black-girl south-side-of-Chicago thing jumped out. "Since it takes two to raise a baby, if you don't want your baby, then neither do I."

I snatched the papers and sat down to complete them. They called my name and off I went—to get an abortion. It was definitely a surreal experience. I had talked about women who had abortions, and I didn't think I'd find my-self in that predicament. Lesson learned—never say never. All I remember is the doctor—this bottle-blonde with her glistening one-carat diamond studs in each ear—between my legs.

When I entered the waiting room expecting to see Steven, he wasn't there. I went into the parking lot to look for the car. It wasn't there. I wanted and needed to lie down. But I had to settle for the waiting room until he re-turned. If I'd still had my apartment, I would have headed home to my own bed at that moment. Oddly, I didn't have any regrets about the abortion. My mother raised me with-out my father, Duke, until Bo Daddy came along my senior year of high school. And while she never complained and my brother Stevie and I never suffered, I wanted to do it differently.

I should have been sitting there viewing Steven differ-ently. Instead, I pulled out my wedding checklist and went over it in the lobby until he returned some forty-five min-utes later.

"Are you okay?" was all he could manage.

"No, are *you* okay? Mission accomplished; baby is gone. You satisfied?"

He avoided the question and asked, "You want to get something to eat?"

"I want to lay down."

"Can we get something right quick?" he asked. "I'm starving."

"What have you been doing for the last five hours?"

"I went to the mall, walked around, and went to the movies," he said.

"I just unexpectedly walked into an office building with a baby, now I'm walking out minus one, and you took your ass to the movies?"

I'm not the cussing type, because I know lots and lots of words. In fact, he accused me of using vocabulary words he didn't understand just to confuse him.

"What else was I going to do all this time?" he whined, trying to assuage my brewing temper.

"Wait!" I said. "Anything could have gone wrong."

"Daaaag, where's your faith?"

"Don't you dare bring God into this conversation that way," I shot back. "I need to lay down."

He had turned the car off and was opening the door for me. I hadn't noticed we were in the parking lot of his favorite steak house. Not only did he not wait for me, but now he was taking me to a steak house when he knew I didn't eat red meat!

Pissed off wasn't even the word. I looked at what I was doing and couldn't believe love had just run off with my heart and my head like that. I was in love with this man down to my core; it was just that simple.

Back at home after our meal in silence I climbed into my pajamas and onto the couch in the living room. Mama Mo kept coming down and finding things to discuss with me. I'd give her short answers because I wasn't much in the mood for talking. I finally asked Steven what he'd bought since he was at the mall for five hours. He said he had purchased things to take on the honeymoon.

Mama Mo made the announcement that night about our honeymoon to Hawaii.

"I will be sending you guys on a fifteen-day, all-inclusive, five-star honeymoon to Hawaii as your wedding gift."

Steven jumped up and hugged her.

"Thank you," I said. "Hawaii is a very expensive place, and fifteen days is a very long time to be away. You don't have to put us up in five-star hotels."

"Oh yes, I do," she said adamantly. "Steven deserves some happiness and I just want to help to make him happy. He's always wanted to go to Hawaii."

Since I had been managing our money, I knew Steven did not have any extra dollars laying around to pay for an abortion. Mama Mo *had* to have been the one who paid for it! It was so in my face at that moment—her sitting there telling me about her baby boy's happiness and me lying there with an empty womb. The juxtaposition of that one almost threw me off the couch.

Lord, please keep me from slapping them both right here, I prayed to myself. But I said "Amen" aloud.

"That's right, Amen," Mama Mo said, figuring I was cosigning her statement about Steven's happiness. "Then it's settled—fifteen days in Hawaii it is!"

I went to bed asking the Lord's forgiveness for what I'd done that day. I also asked him not to punish me by never letting me have a child in the future. I know how He is a forgiving God. I know He had mercy on me. Mercy is something given to you because you don't deserve to have it, an unrestrained exercise of authority, if you will. A song we used to sing at my church in Chicago came flooding back and I whispered the words and fell into a deep sleep.

My mother called me at work to say that Mama Mo had called her to ask if she and Daddy Bo would pay five thousand dollars for us to stay in Hawaii an additional five days.

"Heckie nooooo!" Mommie said. "I told her that La-Joyce has been all over the world, they can go back to Hawaii on their own dime if they like it that much. I have a wedding to pay for."

Mama Mo told her that she was cashing in fifteen thousand dollars of her deceased husband's pension just so we could thoroughly enjoy ourselves and because we would never have this opportunity again.

"I told that woman you would just have to enjoy yourself in fifteen days," my mommie told me. "And that's long enough to be honeymooning, anyway!"

My mother is *not* the one. She takes no tea for the fever. I could only imagine how this conversation had really sounded, with loud, booming "No, ma'am"s. That's *my* mama!

My girlfriends in New York showed up in full force for my bridal shower at our new Brooklyn apartment in Fort Greene. Steven wanted to stay so badly, but it just wasn't right for the groom to be lurking around the women's festivities. He was sure there'd be a stripper. I was disappointed to know he saw me as a stripper kind of girl. My friends know that I'm not, so there was none.

Everyone brought their signature dish and it was on!

The fellowship, the prayers, the gifts—oh, my my my, the gifts! One friend just said aloud, "LaJoyce, you're truly blessed!"

"Yes, I am," I said through tears.

I had been a cohost of a cable television program called *Woman of the Week* for several years, and the executive producer, Miss Lucille, was like a surrogate mother to me. She wanted me feted with her friends who knew me in Miss Lucille style. She was a grand diva with a tremendous amount of style and class. Her gathering was at Dish of Salt, one of New York City's premier Chinese restaurants. Those ladies sent me off with gifts I'd have never considered. Miss Lucille beamed at the success of her party for me. I was humbled and thankful.

Our arrival in Chicago was met with an incredible amount of fanfare from family and friends. The flurry of airport (Midway and O'Hare), Greyhound, and Amtrak arrivals had forced our calendars into a well-coordinated frenzy. Steven and I still had business to take care of at the Cook County clerk's office with the marriage license.

Right there in the county clerk's office, I almost walked away from this dude when he tried to force me into taking his name without a hyphen. That's when I flipped out.

I told that clerk, "You put 'LaJoyce Hunter' and a hyphen before that name!"

"I thought you were really ready to get married. I thought you were old fashioned," he said, trying to lay a guilt trip on me in front of the clerk. Steven had been like a knight in shining armor, rescuing me from my single status at age twenty-eight. I was dangerously in love and ready for a husband, and he knew it.

"I'm both ready to get married and old fashioned, but I will never give up my name totally," I told him, standing my ground on my home turf. "I will, however, add yours. Or . . . we don't have to do this."

The sister-friend clerk looked over her glasses at him for his answer and he just said, "Do whatever you want."

I repeated myself firmly to the clerk, "LaJoyce Hunter *hyphen*."

And that was the end of that.

Our rehearsal at Saint John Church–Baptist was flawless. Tyger was the wedding coordinator and she did a bang-up job. It was surreal being in the same church about to be married by Pastor Johnson, who had christened, baptized, and debutanted me. I sat on the steps leading to the altar watching the rehearsal. It was in that very church that I had gone to Sunday school, sung my first solo in the choir, had my first communion, received my first Bible, gotten my first college scholarship, and spoken from the pulpit for the first time. There was a lot of history for me oozing from those walls. I was about to make another indelible Saint John's imprint in my mind in less than twenty-four hours, and I was getting nervous.

The rehearsal dinner was held at my mother's house, and the food was prepared by her best friend, who I call Aunt Marchita. She cooked my favorite meal—turkey and dressing with a stuffed red snapper. It was just the best-ever festive fellowship. I was pleased to have my two favorite students, Shontisha and Karu, make the journey from New York. Neither of them had ever traveled out of state, and they had a great time enjoying my family.

My best friend in the whole wide world, Tyger, along with my high school buddy and former New York roommate, Kaye, gave me a slam-dunk lingerie bridal shower. Oh, the champagne, the lovely lingerie, and to my surprise a stripper named Tiger! Only Tyger could have dug up such a thing (she knew it wasn't my style, but she didn't care). My friends were so thrilled at his appearance that he didn't even have to bother me!

The next day, my Bo Daddy woke me up to let me know that it was December 1—my wedding day. His calendar said I needed to get to the hairdresser. I was so groggy and fuzzy, probably from too much champagne. Definitely from nervousness. He first had to drive me to Walgreen's, where I bought Pepto-Bismol for the first time in my life and drank it right out of the bottle at the counter to ease my queasiness.

Superstar hairstylist Davvy did the honors at her shop, and I was literally listless as she navigated me from station to station. I kept swigging my bottle of Pepto-Bismol, and I prayed that this feeling in my stomach would pass. I don't know how much time went by, but my Bo Daddy was standing before me as Davvy was flinging off the vinyl cover-up. My hair was glued into an awesome updo that would not come undone unless I washed it.

By the time I got home, I had semi–snapped out of my morning haze. It was a good thing I was all better, because it was sheer bedlam at my house! I gathered all of my things and whispered to Bo Daddy, "Take me to the church."

"Now? So early?" he questioned, since the wedding was at 4 P.M. and it was only noon.

I looked around at the chaos. "Now."

The janitor, whom I've known since I was a kid, was just unlocking the church, and he said, "Now, baby, why you the first one here? Ain't never known no bride to be the first one here."

"I had to leave my house."

"Come on, baby, let's go to your dressing room."

There was a peace that enveloped me sitting all alone in the church where my spiritual foundation was built. I felt home, loved, safe. I cuddled myself up in an old, huge, red velvet pulpit chair in the room and went soundly to sleep for more than an hour.

When I woke up, I immediately went to work on my face. The dramatics of Davvy's updo and Franklin's gown called for my face to be beat—totally made up, replete with lashes. During my makeup application, I kept telling myself not to cry.

You better not ruin this makeup job, girl. It has to last you through the night.

With my makeup, hair, and nap done, I sat in my velvet chair and awaited the arrival of my bridesmaids. They each arrived, rushed and to some extent undone. Their gifts from me were dangling rhinestone earrings with a tiny ball on the end. I had discussed my vision of them wearing updos so we could show off their necklines with those earrings. But who showed with an updo? Only Tyger and my prayer partner Lencola. So I had to comb the hair of my cousin Mayla, Pam, and Steven's two sisters.

Growing up doing dance shows and fashion shows, I was always the resident face painter, and my wedding day was no different. So I had to beat Tyger, Mayla, and Steven's two sisters.

Meanwhile, we got the word that the limo never showed at the hotel for Steven and his crew. Everyone started offering to do this and that.

I didn't even look up.

"Tell them to get a cab," I said calmly. "The hotel is on North Michigan Avenue, this church is on South Michigan Avenue—same street. They'll be here in less than fifteen minutes."

Everyone exhaled; I kept making up my girls.

My early arrival to the church got me centered, calm, rested, and unaffected by the wedding brouhaha that seems to stir just before it begins. I hadn't prayed that the day would be okay; I'd prayed that *I'd* be okay. Ultimately, I knew only God would be in control of the day.

I did not step into my dress until I was absolutely sure we were about to begin. I didn't want one crease in my velvet skirt. We were all flawless! The emerald and ivory velvet with the rhinestone accents shimmered. Mommie and Mama Mo were as beautiful as could be in their fuchsia. My Grannie was beaming and draped with fur and pearls, and Steven's godmother Martha had come all the way from Los Angeles. It was a perfect production.

We made a circle and I asked Lencola to pray. We had

been prayer partners for many years, praying on the phone each morning at 7 A.M. It was only fitting that she bring the group prayer. And pray she did, which sealed the presence of the Holy Spirit and brought a sense of calm to all in the room. I looked at her and winked.

The girls were walking down the aisle to the immaculate voice of my friend from church, Ella, singing Anita Baker's "You Bring Me Joy."

Bo Daddy and I were waiting in the back of the church when I told him, "I've got the strangest feeling I shouldn't be doing this."

He unwrapped my arm from his.

"Who we got to tell?!" he said with his daddy-protect-daughter haughtiness. "Who we got to tell?! See, we can go downtown, have ourselves a party with all that food there, and then I'll take you to Hawaii my damn self!"

"I'm just nervous, c'mon," I recanted, grabbing his arm.

"Yeah, I got your nervous," he said, looking at me sideways.

Just then, I saw my sister-friend Janine and her husband from New York run into the sanctuary to get a seat. They were a solid couple who had endured their share of bumps and curves, but they'd made it. Seeing them helped my calm return and we stepped to the doorway. I honestly had to gasp at the loveliness of the church all aglow with candlelight, emerald, ivory, and rhinestones. I knew a lot of people were trying to make it from New York but I didn't know how many. I was moved to see my new friends there.

My girl Davette had arranged to take the LSATs that day in Chicago just so she could be there, but she didn't know if she'd be finished in time to get to the church. When I saw her, I said aloud, "You made it!" Everyone laughed. I knew the mental gymnastics involved in taking such an exam, and her finishing early meant good-bye record business, hello law school. She had made it in more ways than one.

I saw Steven put on his glasses so he could see me better, because he couldn't see long distances. I had told him not to miss the main event—my walking down the aisle. I'd also told him not to cry because that would make me cry. I didn't want an hour-plus's makeup job on the front of my beaded bodice. Call me vain, but I wanted pretty pictures!

They would absolutely be pretty pictures, because Steven looked *fine* in his brocade-and-velvet jacket. So did the ushers. I hoped my single girlfriends hadn't brought sand to the beach. Stacey was Steven's best man and he was struggling not to cry. He kept inhaling deeply and holding his eyes wide open.

Pastor Johnson asked, "Who gives this bride . . . ?"

Bo Daddy had his chest all puffed out and said, "I do!" Everyone rolled.

Lencola stepped out of the bridesmaids' line to sing the Lord's Prayer. That girl gave the church goosebumps. Her voice soared all up into the rafters of Saint John Church–Baptist and hung out there for the duration of the service.

"Dearly beloved, we are gathered here today . . . ,"
began Pastor Johnson. When he got to the vows part, that's
when I felt as if I'd cry. I held back until I said, "in sickness
and in health." A single tear rolled down my right cheek
and underneath my chin. Steven's eyes welled up and I
shook my head one time and squeezed his hand for him to
hold on.

We made it through with no crying and were off to the
reception. The Guest Quarter Suites had literally decked
the halls for Christmas. It was all so festive; the tone was
set. We danced our first dance to Babyface's "Sunshine,"
which was also an alternative nickname for me other than
Rabbit. While we were dancing, Steven ordered the deejay, my Uncle Johnny, to play a serious jam.

"I got it," Uncle Johnny said.

"I mean, is that a serious jam?" Steven asked, craning
his neck to see the title of what was on the second turn-
table.

Uncle Johnny is a seasoned Chicagoland deejay.

"Man, I got it!" he said.

The first two beats played and everyone there—at least
everyone from Chicago—screamed and jumped out of
their seats and headed to the dance floor. The 1979 dusty
"Love's Gonna Last," by Jeffree, was the song, and it was
such an appropriate first jam song for the crowd. It is a
beloved stepper's cut in Chicago and one that guaranteed
that a party was now under way.

Well, Mr. New York deejay, Steven, had never heard
this song before, and he went straight off! I mean, he went

up to Uncle Johnny and was ordering him to take off the song and put on another. My uncle had to cover his turntables because Steven was reaching for them to snatch the needle off. And here I am, along with my baby brother, Stevie, trying to referee the deejays battling over what was an appropriate jam.

One of my beloved senior family friends gently guided me away from the action to the dance floor, and how could I refuse eighty-three-year-old Mr. Orville? I stepped with him, but I watched. Steven was raving like a lunatic. It was just a record. My brother chilled out the entire situation. I have recently confirmed that Stevie told Steven if he didn't stop showing his behind at his sister's wedding, Stevie'd have it whipped. I had five of my six brothers in the room, my surrogate brother in his full Marine uniform—Master Sergeant Curtis Brookshire—and my daddy. It would not have been pretty.

Steven eventually made up with Uncle Johnny; they laughed about their "creative differences" and we jammed all night. His oldest sister danced so much her dress came undone. She actually pulled the boning out of it and was using it as a dance prop. We hollered! It was truly a beautiful way to begin a new life together. It seemed like the wedding also restored Steven's relationship with his sisters, which had been bitter.

Weddings and funerals—they can bring a family together or tear it apart.

Since we were leaving so early the next morning for Hawaii, we had lots of business to handle before going to sleep. Our honeymoon suite became business office central. Mommie Jo and Mama Mo helped us open all of our gifts. We had several thousand dollars in checks and cash. It took us hours to open them all, record them, endorse the checks, complete deposit slips, and pack. There were little piles at the front door to go to one person or another before we left the hotel. By the time we showered and climbed into bed, we were only going to have two hours of sleep. The consummation of this marriage was going to have to wait.

It took a complete twenty-four hours to get to Hawaii (remind me never to do *that* again). But the journey was well worth it. First stop on our fifteen-day honeymoon was the Mauna Kea Resort in Kona. Can you say mouth-hitting-the-floor luxurious? Truly, a paradise. Their beach was just lovely, and I had packed several books to read during beach and plane time. Steven was furious with me for reading books and reamed me up and down for bringing so many.

"You're not supposed to be reading books on your honeymoon!" He was downright angry.

"We're going to be here fifteen days. I don't want to buy any books," I responded prudently.

By day two, I began getting a clicking in my jaw that made it difficult for me to open and close my mouth, which forced me to call the house doctor.

"Have you been under a lot of stress recently?" he asked.

"Well, I just got married and had a big wedding . . ."

And I have a new husband here acting like a jerk in paradise,
I said to myself.

"That'll do it," he said. "Relax. If you have never had
this thing before, when your stress is minimized, it will go
away. It's called TMJ Disorder. Or lockjaw."

"I'll take that relax part under advisement!" I said.

Steven and I were so exhausted all we did for the first
three days was sleep and eat. We finally got around to con-
summating the marriage on day four. Rest was at the top of
the list.

By day four, I began to wonder who it was I'd married.
Steven visibly started acting differently—making snide
and rude comments about everything I had brought to
wear, how I was combing my hair, what I was eating, my
weight, and yes, my reading books.

I was hearing it from him day and night. It got to the
point where I would tell him I'd be right back and stay
gone for an hour just so I wouldn't have to hear his mouth.
When we were at one restaurant in Maui, Steven was
being so ridiculous to the waiter over an issue that he had
no control over. I was totally embarrassed. I hid my face
and tears streamed freely. The waiter kneeled down to
comfort me, handed me a napkin, and let me know very
loudly he was unfazed by patrons like Steven.

He would always find something to perform over in a
restaurant. I had told him that with so many other people
handling your food, a restaurant is not the place to pick a
fight. Steven embarrassed me in public by treating someone rudely every day. He was acting like a spoiled brat, a

white aristocrat who only knew how to operate from his place of entitlement. Then when he finished reaming Joe Public, he'd turn his venom on me. I cried my eyes out on my honeymoon every day, mainly because I knew I was sleeping with Dr. Jekyll or Mr. Hyde, and I wasn't sure which.

I'm not big on following zodiac signs, but he was a Pisces, and this behavior was that upstream, downstream thing I'd heard people talk about dealing with in Pisces people. Testing the waters for the day to see which way the stream was flowing was apparent in his behavior. I'd have a lot to learn on the subject. Obviously with Steven it was true.

Now, I knew that there was a lot of stress leading up to the wedding, with finding an apartment, finalizing all of the plans, wrapping up at work, but hey . . . here we were in paradise; the drama was supposed to be over.

Little did I know it was just about to unfold.

CHAPTER THREE

The Fire

But his word was in mine heart as a burning fire shut up in my bones, and I was weary with forbearing, and I could not stay.

—JEREMIAH 20:9

On December 18, we finally arrived back in New York. Mama Mo met us at JFK Airport and drove us to Long Island to get our car. I was so exhausted, but I wanted and needed to get to my own bed. I had to work the next day.

Steven had simmered down considerably. I knew the stress of it all had him acting cuckoo-for-cocoa-puffs! Mama Mo talked to him for hours about each detail of the trip. Talking to her seemed to take the edge off for him. I thought to myself, *So Mama Mo is the secret weapon to chilling him out. Got it!*

Back at work, the word had already circulated in the industry about the loveliness of our wedding. There were so many people to talk to, but I had already been away from home and work for twenty days. Mental note: never do that again.

At 2 A.M. on Friday, December 21, we got a phone call from an operator asking for Steven to take a number and call his younger sister.

"What has she gotten herself into now?" he questioned as he dialed the number.

When he spoke to her I only heard, "What's up . . . when? . . . how did that happen? . . . is? . . . ," and then a scream that was stuck in his throat and didn't come out of his open mouth.

I pried the phone away from his white knuckles.

"What happened?" I asked his sister.

The news threw me back onto the bed.

There had been a fire at the house in Long Island. His oldest sister had had to jump out of the window on fire and was now at the hospital. Mama Mo was dead.

"Dead?" I repeated.

"Yes, dead. Hurry up and get out here," she said calmly.

I picked up on her calm. "We're on the way."

Sweet Jesus! I thought.

Steven had fallen onto the floor by the bathroom and was pounding it, screaming, "Who am I going to tell all my secrets to now? Who am I going to talk to? My mother is dead! She was so good; she shouldn't be the one dead!"

I hugged him until his crying ceased.

"Your sisters need you," I said. "I know things haven't always been great between you guys, but you need to stick together now more than ever, and they need you to be strong."

I said a quick prayer with him for our strength, and

while he washed, I laid out his clothes. We were out of the house in fifteen minutes. From the car I called my parents.

"We're on the way," my mother said.

Next call, Godmother Martha in California. Only a machine. Steven wanted me to leave a message.

"No way! Don't ever leave such a terrible message on someone's machine," I advised.

He agreed.

The most bizarre thing happened while he was driving; he was struck with road rage and began trying to hit another car.

"Man, my mother just died," he yelled at the dude in the other car from his rolled-down window. "I ain't got nothing to lose. Just give me a reason!"

"Stop!" I screamed. "Stop the car right now!"

He didn't listen. He kept gunning for the man in the other car. Finally, the guy turned off the street and we drove top-speed to Long Island.

When we got there it was a scene like something you'd dream—firemen were everywhere, still trying to put out the fire. There were also policemen and investigators, because there was a dead body in the house, so it was officially a crime scene. The house was charred to a crisp. I threw up as soon as I got close. Steven's knees buckled as he ran toward the house calling his mother. Some of his neighbors helped him up and to a seat on the porch across the street. I had gotten a bad case of the shakes. My teeth were chattering and the tears kept pouring down my face.

Their neighbor, Mr. Ingraham, recalled how he tried to

save Mama Mo when Steven's baby sister ran to his house with her three-year-old son. He said he got his ladder and put it up to Mo's bedroom window. He opened the window and he could hear her screaming. He told her to come closer to his voice, to climb out of the window, and that he was there to get her out. She kept screaming and he kept talking until the pressure from the fire blew out the window and cut his head open.

"I had to come down then," he conceded, sadly pointing to his patched-up head. I threw up again.

Day was just beginning to break and I remember thinking how beautifully orange the clouds in the sky were as the sun promised its ascent. I was shivering so much, Mrs. Ingraham silently ushered me to her bedroom, flipped back her covers, took off my shoes, shoved me down, and covered me up. I cried to myself as God said to me, "Don't let Me go."

Two days back from the honeymoon, married only twenty-one days. Wow, it was clear to me that His hand was the only one worth holding.

After my nap, we arrived at the hospital to check on Steven's older sister. She had second- and third-degree burns on her face, hands, arms, and the back of her head. Fortunately for her, she had fallen asleep in a wool dress and a robe. When she was awakened by the screams of her mother, she had jumped out of the window from the second floor of their split-level ranch home.

She was in need of skin grafting and hours of therapy, and had to be transported immediately to the burn unit at another hospital. Just as we were entering the hallway from the emergency room, the paramedics were rolling in Mama Mo in a black body bag.

Steven made the announcement, "They're bringing her in now."

I threw up again.

And Steven shook his head and rushed to help me. A watchful nurse asked him how many times had I done so.

"Ever since she got to the house this morning," he answered, concerned.

The nurse took me into a room, rolled up my sleeve, and pricked me with an IV needle.

"You're dehydrated, miss," she informed me as I looked up at the bag of saline drip. "Here, drink this."

She handed me a bottle of orange-flavored Gatorade. I watched listlessly as the drip ran into my arm while Steven ran around the hospital checking on his sisters, collecting paperwork, and being a good big brother.

The hospital was packed with family and friends from the neighborhood when I finally got off of my drip, which had been just what I needed. Now I could be of some help to everyone. We saw a cute, petite woman rushing toward us, and Stacey's wife, Claudette, said, "Is that . . . Darlene?" The woman got closer.

"Yep, it sure is," Claudette laughed nervously.

Darlene was Steven's ex-wife. I thought it was a friendly gesture for her to show up. Steven's eyes bugged out of his head when he saw her. He hurriedly walked toward Darlene and turned her around in the other direction. They stood talking for a while and I saw him pointing to me. I heard her say she was really happy for him, but she was sorry about what happened and to let her know the funeral's date.

His sister had such a long recovery time ahead of her, so it was decided that the funeral would be a memorial whenever she was able to attend a service.

My parents rolled into LaGuardia Airport that night, as promised, with helpful hands ready. My mother could see I had done a lot of crying and I didn't want to cry in front of her. Bo Daddy, Steven, and other men searched through the house to see what they could salvage. They brought back garbage bags full of papers, clothes, and photos.

Steven unzipped a black garment bag that had my wedding gown in it. That's right, Mama Mo brought it back with her from Chicago. The night we arrived from the honeymoon, she had asked me if I wanted to take the gown with me. Steven told her we'd be back over the weekend to get everything.

When I saw my gown all charred, I lost it.

"Zip it up!" I cried. "Just throw it out!"

I felt a terrible pit in my stomach that I couldn't quite explain.

My mother was on paper duty, sorting and filing important papers that would be necessary for these children to piece together their past. It needed a meticulous eye and she was the right one for the job. My mother quietly called me over to read a yellow slip that was burned a bit in places, but still legible in others.

"Look at this." She eyed me as I read.

My eyebrow went up at the hospital receipt for an HIV antibody test. It had Steven's name handwritten across the top. My mother and I gave each other a quizzical look. She pushed and pointed me in Steven's direction and continued to look through the paperwork—with one eye up and both ears open, no doubt.

I cornered Steven in the music room.

"Mommie found this," I said handing him the paper.

He barely looked at it, yet he knew exactly what it was.

"Everybody's had a test at some point. It's nothing," he assured me, and put the paper in his pocket with a kiss.

I sat back down and continued to go through the bags with my mother. We didn't mention it again until he left.

"Well . . . ?" my mother inquired.

"He said it's a test he took because everyone has taken one."

"Have you?"

"No."

"Me neither," she said flippantly.

"If we would have gotten married in New York, it's state law to take a blood test before marriage. But because we got married in Chicago, it was not a requirement."

"Humph, we'll see," Mommie said.

Meanwhile, the wedding video had arrived to a lackluster reception. None of us wanted to look at it with Mama Mo now dead. I watched it by myself first.

The videographer captured the wedding party's salutations. Steven's older sister said, "I want you all to have a good trip to Hawaii. Welcome to the family, LaJoyce. You just don't know, you're taking a lot off our hands, chile!"

The younger sister said, "Congratulations, you guys. LaJoyce, he's your problem now; don't send him back to our house!"

Mama Mo had wished us congratulations and ended her salutation with "See, Steven, I told you about all of that worrying. Everything always works out in the end," and two winks of the eye.

What was that all about? I thought to myself.

I did notice how reverent Mama Mo was during Lencola's rendition of "The Lord's Prayer." Her hands were folded and she was totally prayerful and pensive.

I started to think about things she had said that were beginning to make sense: "Don't wait to get married," "I'm sending you to Hawaii because you'll never have this chance again," and her quiet praise during "The Lord's Prayer." Did she know something was going to happen to her?

When Steven's older sister did get out of the hospital a month later, we finally held Mama Mo's memorial service. Godmother Martha came from California and spoke at the service, where she admitted the two of them hadn't seen one another in twenty years before our wedding.

"We ran up and down the hall all night to each other's rooms, giggling and sharing secrets just like when we were young girls," she said from the pulpit.

The church was packed and it was quite a somber occasion.

Steven and his sisters didn't have a lot of time to discuss plans for their future. During these conversations, it
was them against him. They had hateful, heated discus-
sions with nasty words flying at each other. One thing was
clear: there was no way—even with their mama dead and
the home they grew up in burned to a crisp—the three of
them would ever again live under the same roof. When I
suggested it, they all looked at me as if I'd lost my mind.
Honestly, to marry into this mess, maybe I had. It is said
that death brings out the worst in people. And the three of
them were a hot mess. (No pun intended.)

I had to call my little brother, Stevie, in Chicago and
make him vow that under *no* circumstances would we act
like that when the day came to bury our mother. I made
him promise that we'd make her proud even in her death.
Because these children were acting like urchins who had
never been raised right.

Mama Mo had worked as a nurse—at night, to get the
higher pay rate—when her husband died years earlier. She
saved and gave her three children the best—maybe too
much of it. Seeing them argue so viciously with one another made me sick.

"You all have too much business to sort out and lots of
decisions to make," I said, trying to referee. "You're going to
have to leave the past in the past to accomplish anything."

Three months later, they were finally able to collect on
Mama Mo's insurance policy, tear down the house, and
sell the land. This brought in a considerable amount of
cash to be divided among the three of them.

Steven said he wanted to get out of New York State. I was all for that, because I had been five months away from going back to Chicago when we met. New York had gotten all of the rent from me I intended to pay. In the eight years I had lived in New York, I spent $384,000 in rent! There was no way I wanted to dish out another dime, and I didn't want to buy a house there because the taxes were just too ridiculous. That, in my mind, was too many new pairs of shoes and trips to places where I could see my feet in the bottom of blue water.

So, with a new checking account full of cash, Steven's first stop was the travel agency. We sat there for many hours perusing brochures. I knew he wanted to go to the Caribbean, so I focused on that.

"What's the name of that place in Jamaica you guys at work did a live broadcast from with Donnie Simpson?" he asked, totally interested.

"We've been to Jamaica fifteen times," I said. "Which place?"

"The one that you said was the ultimate in swanky."

"The Grand Lido? That place costs a fortune!" Always my prudence came first.

"That's the one!" he said, beaming, and turned to the agent and announced, "The Grand Lido in Negril, please."

She smiled and handed him the brochure.

When we left the travel agency, Steven had booked us first-class trips to Virginia Beach, Atlanta, Charlotte, Los Angeles, a Mexican Caribbean cruise to join my parents' annual jaunt, and yes, Negril's Grand Lido. He wrote that woman a check for $20,000! I was absolutely flabbergasted.

"What's the occasion?" the agent wanted to know. Funny how when you spend a few dollars with people it gives them license to be all in your business.

Steven would tell anyone who would listen to his story. "My mother just died and I deserve some happiness. My new wife and I are going to see the world."

He had lots of time at his job to take these trips. He told me I could take off without pay. The pay wasn't the point. Who was going to write my programs? The career I had as a writer and producer wasn't just some job where my boss could call a temp agency and get a replacement, nor could they snatch a secretary to sit in my chair during my absence. So many days off meant putting a lot of strain on the other two writers and producers.

"Steven, I have to think about my job, and this kind of money could be a down payment on our house."

"You're a wife now, not just some radio industry hustler," he said. "You don't even really have to work."

"Industry hustler?! . . ." I started to get pissed, but he shut me up with a kiss.

"I got it like that now," he said. "My mother wanted me to be happy with you. We're not going to get this opportunity again. Case closed."

I was pissed to the nth degree. "Don't you ever call me an industry hustler again. I've worked my tail off in this business; I don't appreciate you minimizing my career."

One month later Steven got his wish. Sheridan Broadcasting Networks was moving its production unit to Pittsburgh. If I wanted to go there I could, but otherwise, I was laid off with one month's pay and the ability to collect unemployment. I was the first in my department to go, and the others would follow in two months.

I had never seen my husband so happy as when he found out that his wife didn't have a job. He was strange like that. Some things elated him, and nonissue things sent him raging. He went out that night and bought me all sorts of things to set up my home office.

"You're going into business," he announced. "Look at how God worked out you being able to take all of our trips!"

"Yeah, look at that," I mused.

I also noted that he conveniently thanked God when it suited him. He praised God when things were going his way. I'd been a reader of the Word for a long time and I knew that it was not my place to question Steven's salvation or the salvation he claimed to have. However, when you begin to come to church with me just to monitor the amount of money I'm putting into the collection plate, questions arise. I'm not exactly prying, but I'm definitely wondering.

For once, we agreed the business would be great, especially since it didn't take all that much money to get me started with Retnuh Relations (Hunter is my maiden name, Retnuh, inverted). We specialized in publicity, production, and programming. The production part meant radio, television, and event production. With my additional phone line installed, I was officially in business, with more clients than I could handle.

One of my largest clients was the New York Urban League. We were responsible for coordinating the entertainment aspects and all publicity for their annual Whitney Young Football Classic, held at Giants Stadium. My team of four did an awesome job of generating hundreds of press hits and creating a tailgate party with live entertainment from chart-topping artists. Superstars Will Downing and Eric Gable rendered "The Star-Spangled Banner" and "Lift Every Voice and Sing."

I had been working day and night on this event, and on the big day I needed to be at the stadium very early. Steven decided for me that I didn't need to be there so early because in his mind I had done enough for the event but hadn't done enough as a wife while working on this project. He wanted us to hang pictures on the wall in our apartment. He then gathered the pictures he wanted hung, got the hammer and nails, and solicited my help.

"Steven, I need to be at the stadium in ninety minutes, are you taking me?" I asked, calm as you please.

"Nope. Not until you take care of some of your wifely duties around here!" he ranted. "Are you helping me or not?!"

"Not today. I've got a show to do," I said, temper still in check, sarcasm roaring.

I called Mikey, my teammate, play brother, and former Sheridan Broadcasting office mate and producer, to pick me up. I washed my hair right quick, left Steven a ticket to enter the stadium, and went outside to sit on the stoop to wait for Mikey. Calm. I had a show to do.

Steven showed up at the stadium right at kickoff. I

was soaring over the record-number attendance that we had helped to attain. And the first-ever tailgate party was a smash. I cuddled Steven's arm and said, "Isn't this great!"

My prayer partner, Lencola, sat next to Steven and listened to him complain about my unwifely actions of the day. She reminded him that he was the one who wanted me in business.

"This is her business," she said waving her arms around, pointing to every corner of the stadium. "After this—and because of the success today, there will be an 'after this'—it's on to the next event."

Thank you, prayer partner. Well said, I thought. *Amen.*

Steven and I spent most of 1991 taking the trips Steven had booked around the country. And we had a ball! We were in active pursuit of finding a new city to live in. When we got to Charlotte, Virginia Beach, and Atlanta, we'd be picked up by a Realtor who would spend a couple of days showing us around their city. These places were very lovely, but none of them excited me enough to make me want to move there. Steven loved hot weather, and I loved cold weather and the drastic change in seasons.

Claudette and Stacey were taking a lot of quick trips to the Poconos in the mountains of Pennsylvania and invited us to their family home one weekend. They had a wonderful chalet at the end of a narrow dirt road along a raging creek that Stacey's father had bought some twenty years before after getting a view of it from a helicopter.

The Poconos were beautiful, with lush vegetation that

you could smell, free-roaming deer, raccoons, beaver, bob-cats, wild turkeys, and bears. Steven was so relaxed in the Poconos atmosphere that he wanted to come back. So did I. Stacey agreed that anytime they came back we had a standing invitation to join them. Oh, the times we had in that chalet!

On our rides up following Stacey on Friday nights, Steven and I created a song that started out as a whisper: "We're going to the Poconos." A little louder, "We're going to the Poconos." A little louder, "We're going to the Po-conos!" Screaming, *"We're going to the Poconos!"*

One three-day weekend up there, with perfect weather to welcome us back, Steven was out exploring while Sta-cey and Claudette were having a major disagreement. As usual, I tried to referee, because I could see this was about to spiral out of control. Just as I saw it spiraling, Stacey made the announcement, "Pack up, everybody, I'm closing the house!"

I knew not to play with Stacey. I got up, packed our stuff, and put it at the front door to wait for everyone else to get moving. Steven came back hours later whistling and carrying a pizza. He almost tripped over the bags at the door; he looked at me and I shrugged.

In the car I said, "I don't want to go back to Brooklyn today."

"Me either," he said. "Let's just drive around and see what all is here."

We got a motel room and set off on a mountain adven-ture, turning down roads we had never been on before that day. What we discovered were all of these communities tucked away where people lived full time. It was very interesting. The permanent resident homes were very different from the vacation houses.

Sunday afternoon, a Realtor was asking us what we wanted to see in a vacant lot where we would one day build our home. I spoke up first. "Seclusion, acreage, and water on the property."

Steven nodded his approval.

"I've got just the place," she said. "It's a little ride, so let's go."

The property was so all the way up the mountain that I was in the backseat getting carsick. There were so many turns, I was thinking, *This place is out, because I can't make the ride.*

The property was on a dead-end dirt road at the top of the mountain, but in a ridge with a stream winding through its three acres. I perched myself on a rock and looked around.

"This is it!" Steven exclaimed to me and the Realtor.

"Yep, it is."

"How much?" I asked.

She looked at her papers. "Wow, this property is in foreclosure!"

I looked at Steven; we did our special move and touched our pointer fingers together as if we were slapping high-five.

I sat right there on that rock praising God aloud because it seemed like we were right up there next to Him.

Within the hour, we had purchased that property and qualified for the payment plan, with the objective of building a house on it whenever we were ready.

We sang our little ditty the rest of the weekend, changing "going" to "moving." "We're *moving* to the Poconos . . ."

All of my projects had wrapped up for the year and I didn't want to just sit around from October until January with nothing to do. I went to work as a supervisor at TicketMaster. It was an easy, pay-every-week gig and just the thing I needed to keep me busy. But I was devastated to find that I had to work on Christmas Day. Why in the world a ticket center would be open on Christmas Day, I'll never know. Steven blew a gasket, going off about my hours.

We were supposed to enjoy the day in Queens at his cousin Charles's house. Charles was the patriarch of their family, and although he was a cousin, he was more like an uncle. I called him Uncle Charles then and still do today. Steven didn't feel that it was right for him to spend his first Christmas without his mother and without his wife, too.

I understood, but I was already committed until 5 P.M.

"Go on to Queens and I'll meet you there," I told him.

He didn't want to do it because he and his sisters still had a mess brewing between them a year after Mama Mo died.

I took all the money I had earned at TicketMaster and bought Steven an expensive piece of mixing equipment to aid in the production of *Quiet Storm* Japan, the show he produced for WBLS on-air personality Vaughn Harper. I also bought him a blue-jean jacket airbrushed with my headshot in color on the back with "My Sunshine" scripted above it. Master artist Ricco, who did tour clothes for the stars, created it for him. The front had "Steve" written on one side and his Masonic emblem on the other. He didn't know when he was going off that I spent all of my money on him.

By the end of my shift at TicketMaster, the call volume was so low that they paid more for the staffing than they had earned for the day. I believe the main purpose of my working there was to meet Ruth and her husband Clive, who was a computer repairman for Xerox.

Ruthie and Clive became like Claudette and Stacey to us. We three couples would have an incredible ball on a regular basis. Ruthie and I both got fired from Ticket-Master right when Retnuh Relations was gearing up again. My ego was a little bruised at getting fired from a twenty-thousand-dollar-a-year job that I only wanted to work for a short time anyway. The Holy Spirit reminded me that "ego" equals Easing God Out. *Get over it.* So I did.

Business was booming and Ruthie became my assistant. She had so many talents that were being wasted on the phones at TicketMaster, I quickly discovered. I was a master organizer, but Ruthie was the master-blaster organizer! Clive, who we dubbed "Mr. Computer Man," was a closet wannabe record producer. We all went to several record company parties and showcases together. He was so sweet that if I could help him get put on, great.

Clive had a computer purchasing program at his company through Macintosh, and he got me my very first Macintosh so I could write all of the books I talked about and get them off of legal pads and out of my journals.

Steven and Clive discovered that they shared a love for guns and range shooting. Steven carried a gun with him all the time. He had many friends who were New York City policemen and he had a little courtesy shield from someone, too.

Sometimes, Steven would act like he was a policeman if there was trouble in the street. I walked away from him trying to control a situation in our subway station one evening when we came home from a party. Maybe it was the alcohol, of which he drank too much. All I know is that my Steven was no policeman and had no business trying to control a potentially dangerous situation as if he were one. I literally ran home, because I couldn't stand to see the repercussions that may have arisen from his bravado. My mother always said, "When you see trouble, go the other way."

Steven and Clive went to buy shotguns, and we took a long ride to the end of Long Island for a day trip to a shooting range in Montauk. They got Ruthie and me all set up with our ear mufflers and shooting target sheets twenty feet away. Ruthie barely hit the paper and we all cheered her on in fun.

I hit the target bull's-eye and Steven rejoiced, "Good, Rabbit! I'm gonna move it back ten more feet. See if you can hit it, okay?"

Bull's-eye.

"You've got beginner's luck today, honey," he said.

"Something like that," I confessed.

Ten more feet back and bull's-eye. And again, and again. Finally, at about a hundred feet back, with a little crowd gathering, I slammed it again. Steven was visibly rattled.

Someone behind me asked, "What are you, some kind of marksman?"

I reloaded the rifle. "Uh-huh," I said, and quickly changed the subject.

"Here, honey, it's your turn," I said, handing everything over to Steven as if nothing had happened.

He stared at me sideways and sat down with a "why didn't you tell me" look. He didn't have a clue I had such skill. With a husband who made schizophrenic behavior a regular practice, being a sure shot is a little something a girl may want to keep to herself.

My Grannie taught me how to shoot a gun out of the window into her backyard. Every time I went to her house, at night we'd shoot her .45 Smith & Wesson. She had a generous backyard in a noisy neighborhood where gunshots were not unfamiliar. She would say, "Hit this in the yard, hit that."

During the day she would set up various objects and at night we'd shoot them from the window. She taught me the foolproof way to shoot with the skill of a marksman, no matter how far away your target.

I'd go to a range with friends through the years and my

love for rifles grew, as did my skill. I've never been certified a marksman, but the marksman in me was evident just the same that day when Steven found out something else about me.

He and I moved to a large duplex apartment in a brownstone nearby in Clinton Hills, Brooklyn. It was absolutely awesome, with two bedrooms and three bathrooms. And it ought to have been for sixteen hundred dollars monthly, not including utilities. All of our friends helped us do a one-day move. We provided pizza, pop, and junk food. It took us only about five hours to be totally moved in from six blocks away.

While we didn't have any children, we adopted my former student, Karu. He stayed almost every weekend at our house, even though he lived three subway stops away, also in Brooklyn. The two of us got off to a rocky start when I was his journalism teacher, but when I promised to call his mother—and did—about his classroom behavior, he did an about-face.

Karu was a budding journalist and considered me his mentor, which was an honor because he had a special gift for writing and reporting entertainment news. He was a bright spot for me and Steven, and though he was a college-age young man, Karu was wise beyond his years. We adored his company and he was a great team member for all Retnuh Relations projects. He kept Steven rolling and his spirits high. It was a man thing. I knew Karu would grow up to become an awesome player in the entertainment industry and with his internet column "The Ru Report," which had more than 300,000 readers. (He has since retired from doing the report.)

Nowadays, he's not just my former student but a colleague, Pocono neighbor, and friend.

I had begun a massive project with the National Black Leadership Commission on AIDS to coordinate their first-ever Choose Life Benefit Gospel Concert. I had to procure an all-star talent roster, gospel and secular, to perform for the benefit to be held at Abyssinian Baptist Church. Additionally, there were pre- and post-receptions, all to be put into motion by me. It was a huge undertaking, but I love huge projects. My team members were in place and we went to work.

The CEO and founder of the organization, Debra Fraser-Howze, is an incredible visionary; she could dream as big as I could execute. She and I were an unstoppable team. Debra became like a big sister to me. Our families are like family to one another even to this day, and it all came about from what she saw at the Urban League game the day Steven wanted pictures hung in our apartment.

With an awesome team in place, I felt comfortable enough to take a trip out to California. First stop was Godmother Martha's; then we visited my childhood buddy Dawn Keith, a then-budding comedienne and actress. Steven wasn't feeling well when we got to her house and she ordered him to lie down for a nap while we went for groceries.

"What's wrong with that baby?" Dawn quizzed me.

"I'm not sure, he came down with some bug and he's had the runs all morning."

"What's wrong with that baby?" she asked me again, stopping the car to look me in the face.

I looked at her strangely. Dawn was the drama queen of our bunch, but I didn't have a clue.

"We've been friends since we were teenage girls and there ain't no secrets between us." She exhaled deeply. "I guess you'll tell me when you're ready."

I didn't know what Dawn was talking about, but for some reason T. D. Jakes was in the back of my mind preaching, "Get ready! Get ready! Get ready!"

CHAPTER FOUR

The Diagnosis

*No weapon that is formed against thee shall
prosper; and every tongue that shall rise against
thee in judgment thou shalt condemn.*

*This is the heritage of the servants of the Lord,
and their righteousness is of me, saith the Lord.*

—ISAIAH 54:17

By the time we arrived at our last stop of the Los Angeles tour, Steven was visibly sick and he refused to go to the doctor. He kept taking over-the-counter drugs to ease the symptoms that had seized him. The medicine he was taking did help some. He'd feel well enough to get dressed up and go to all of the activities we'd arranged, but by nightfall he'd be sick again.

We had planned a dinner at the home of legendary radio personality Frankie Crocker right before we left to get on the red-eye flight back to New York. Steven had taken really sick at a Sony Music party, and we had to leave Los Angeles early. Frankie was very disappointed, because he liked Steven and was looking forward to hosting us at his home.

Frankie was like a father to me in the industry. I wrote scripts for him twice for events, and he bragged that I was the only person industry-wide who could put words in his mouth. That was the ultimate compliment from Frankie Crocker the Chief Rocker!

We had booked tickets on the red-eye because we both wanted to go to work directly from the airport. Steven called in sick and stayed in bed all day. I tried to get him to go to the doctor but he flatly refused. I whipped up a homemade soup and fresh bread for dinner. Soups and bread from scratch take forever to make with all of the chopping, dicing, and kneading involved.

Steven woke up hungry and followed his nose to the kitchen. When I saw him I almost passed out. He was visibly blue!

"How are you feeling?" I asked nonchalantly, not wanting to alarm him.

"Not that great," he said. "But I'm hungry."

I served him up some piping hot chicken noodle vegetable soup.

"And when you finish that we're going to the emergency room," I said. "It's time you got some real medicine and found out what was wrong with you."

"I don't want to go tonight," he said adamantly. "I'll go in the morning."

I took his hands in mine so I could look at his fingertips. They were blue. His oxygen wasn't circulating properly.

"My mother always said never go to an emergency room at night because the better doctors work days," he offered. "So I'll go in the morning and we'll drive out to Mercy Hospital in Long Island. I always promised my mother that if I got sick, I'd go to the hospital where she worked."

"We'll go wherever you want, just as long as you go," I said, wondering if he would make it through the night.

Steven wanted to take a bath and we had a huge whirlpool tub for two. He hated baths and had never even been in it. I drew the water, but he said he was too weak to walk downstairs to get into it.

"Rabbit, draw me another bath up here."

He was beginning to scare me, asking for things he'd never wanted before—first a bath, and then one in the guest bathroom? He soaked in the tub for a couple of hours, letting out the cold water and running more hot. When he called me to help him out, his lips were blue and he was shaking, even though the bathroom was a sauna.

"Are you sure you don't want to go to the emergency room now?" I said. "We can go to Lenox Hill in the city."

"No! I want to go to Mercy," he pleaded. "I don't want to go to New York."

"Okay, okay, okay," I conceded.

"Help me, I just want to lay down."

He refused the pajamas, asking for a sweatsuit instead. I got him dressed, laid him on the couch in the living room, and covered him up.

Downstairs, I called Godmother Martha, who is a nurse, about what was happening with him.

"Watch him through the night," she ordered. "Take him to the hospital first thing in the morning, don't delay."

I set the clock every hour and got up to check on him because I was so jet-lagged from California I didn't trust myself to wake up.

By morning, Steven was listless and even more visibly blue; his lips were crusted over and his eyes were all glassy. He had no strength to even get to the car. I called our neighbor, Dewanda, for help getting him into the car. She looked at me with a "what happened to him" stare. I shrugged; I didn't know.

In the emergency room, his vitals were all too low and they started plugging him up for monitoring, poking him to administer an IV for his dehydration. He was going to be tested for every possible thing, and that meant being admitted to the hospital.

A robust black man came in to introduce himself as Steven's doctor. We shot each other a "thank you, Jesus" glance.

The doctor pulled up a chair to get eye-level with Steven, who was lying down on the bed.

He got right to it.

"Have you ever been diagnosed with HIV?" he asked.

Steven's eyes got as big as a deer's in headlights.

"No, why would you say that?" he asked.

"Well, I'm not sure, but all of your symptoms point to that or some kind of cancer."

"Cancer?" we echoed like parakeets.

"I'm only speculating here, you guys," the doctor said. "But all symptoms point to something very, very serious. You're going to be here awhile until we find out exactly what that is."

On September 12, 1992, my husband of two years was being tucked away in a Long Island hospital for I didn't know how many days until they uncovered the underlying cause of his symptoms. I had to switch gears back to businesswoman because I still had a show to do for an incredibly awesome cause.

I turned thirty on September 24. Tyger flew in just so we could go to an all-you-can-eat lobster feast. I took her with me to the hospital to visit Steven. Two weeks into his stay and they were still fuzzy on what exactly was wrong with him. He had a card and flowers for my birthday.

Relishing their loveliness, I still tried to be prudent.

"I hope you didn't buy these flowers in the lobby, because they cost too much down there," I commented. Tyger pinched me in the back. "They're beautiful!" I exclaimed in my do-over. "Thank you, honey!"

"Take my Rabbit out for a nice dinner since I can't, okay?" Steven said, handing Tyger an envelope.

"I promise," she said, hugging him. "You get better fast; my best girlfriend needs you."

At dinner Tyger commented, "Steven looks bad, LaJoyce. What kind of hospital is this that they don't know what's wrong with him?"

"I know, and it's been two weeks already. He won't go to another hospital."

"Maybe he just wants to stay there in honor of his mother."

"I thought so, too," I said. "That's why I'm not pressing him. But they need to tell me something soon. Sleeping in a lounge chair and then driving to the city for work is really killing me."

"Don't say that, girl, 'cause you ain't dead yet," she said, raising her glass. "Happy birthday."

The very next day at the National Black Leadership Commission on AIDS (BLCA) office, Steven's doctor called to say my husband was being relocated to the intensive care unit because he had a fever of 104 that wouldn't go down and that I should get there ASAP. I started crying.

"Doctor, have you come up with a diagnosis yet?" I asked through tears.

"Well, there are still several more tests to be done, like . . ." And he named everything under the sun, except what I was listening for.

I interrupted him. "Have you tested him for AIDS?"

"Well, you can't just test people for AIDS," he said. "I mean, you need consent, and then there is a whole counseling component, and—"

I interrupted him with a fit of screams and tears, but I was very focused.

"You have had my husband in the hospital for two weeks and have no clue what is wrong with him!" I said. "If there is a possibility he may have AIDS, then you could have tested him and counseled him by now!"

Debra appeared in the doorway listening to the ruckus, feeding me tissues and agreeing with me. That doctor didn't know that I was sitting at *the* premier black agency for policy on AIDS in the nation. He didn't want me to put

Debra on the phone. She was just waiting for the opportunity to pounce on him with her title as a member of the Presidential Advisory Council on AIDS. I wanted the doctor chewed up, but not like Debra would have given it to him.

"Test my husband for AIDS today and don't let me ask you again!" I ordered. Debra offered great comfort and sent me on my way, and I jumped on the subway to Brooklyn and then got in my car.

While I was driving the Holy Spirit said to me, "Open your hands." I looked at the brewing traffic jam, balanced my palms on the wheel, and stretched open my fingers. I felt an incredibly warm sensation going through them, and I praised God right there for the anointing that He was giving me. When I got to the hospital, I knew exactly what to do.

Steven was in the ICU drinking chocolate milk.

"Rabbit, you're not supposed to be here today. Don't make Debra mad," he teased.

If he only knew what had happened earlier. I kissed his head but I didn't say anything. I was speaking in the Spirit under my breath as I flipped back the covers. I rubbed his feet, legs, thighs, belly, arms, and up to his ears.

"That was a drive-by massage," I said. "You'll be better soon. I love you."

I kissed his forehead and left. On my way out, I told the nurse on duty to contact me at work when his fever went down and left her the number. We had an all-nighter to pull for the event. I bounced out of the building singing a song of praise. Two hours later at the office the hospital called to say that Steven was back in his room and that his temperature had stabilized. *Hallelujah!*

The First Annual Choose Life Benefit Gospel Concert went off without a hitch on October 12, 1992, at the Abyssinian Baptist Church in Harlem. The lineup included Donnie McClurkin, Ashford & Simpson, Tramaine Hawkins, Donald Malloy, and Elder Timothy Wright and his choir. The host was Clifton Davis and the sermon was delivered by the Reverend Jesse Jackson.

Tyger and her brother Ronnie flew in specially to be with me for this black-tie affair, which turned out to be an absolute sold-out success. Donald Malloy brought the house down. As I was listening, I was thinking about Steven. I excused myself from the sanctuary and ran to the stairwell to cry. Donald had ushered in a new realm of the Holy Spirit that grabbed hold of me and wouldn't let go.

Bishop Sam Williams, with whom I cohosted a gospel radio show for several years, and Tyger saw me run out and they both came to comfort me. The presence of the Holy Spirit was comforting me at that moment, and so did my anointed and appointed friends there encircling me.

Godmother Martha flew in to see about the situation firsthand. My telephone reports were no longer satisfactory. Being a nurse, she came in and completely took over at the hospital and my kitchen. I was barely eating and she made me the best food ever. We had a different steamed fish every night. She made me come home for dinner instead of camping out at the hospital.

I had seen Steven get pricked, poked, and prodded in every direction. When they tapped into his spinal column to drain fluid and took a piece of bone out of his spine, my goose was cooked. I didn't need to see all of *that*. Bearing witness to the awesome healing machine God made of the body convinced me to continue to take good care of myself.

The next day, the family was going to an emergency meeting called by the doctor at the hospital. After forty days in the hospital, it was confirmed finally that Steven had pneumonia. I told Debra the diagnosis and she summoned me to a behind-closed-doors conversation in the conference room at the office.

"Have the doctors mentioned the term 'PCP' to you?" Debra asked, concerned.

"No, because I don't know what that is."

"It stands for 'Pneumocystis carinii pneumonia,'" she explained. "It is in association with people who are HIV positive. I need you to brace yourself for what the doctors will tell you tomorrow. And I need you to call me the minute after you meet with them."

Brace myself?

The scripture from Psalm 18 showed up in my face plain as day: *He is a buckler to all those that trust in Him.*

I could only brace myself if I had something to hold on to. Jesus had been my rock thus far, and he'd be my brace now.

The meeting invitees at the hospital were Godmother Martha, Uncle Charles, and me. The doctor called me into Steven's room alone and sat down. I sat on the edge of the bed and held Steven's hand.

"Rabbit, I just want to let you know that your husband has AIDS," Steven said. He wanted to be the one to tell me.

Jesus was holding me up. Braced. I hugged Steven tightly, but I didn't cry. I looked over at the doctor for answers only he could provide.

"Steven is not just HIV positive," the doctor said. "He has full-blown AIDS. Currently, his T-cell count is four. A healthy person has a T-cell count of twelve hundred to fifteen hundred. When he walked into the emergency room, Steven was on his way out. At this point we need to get him on a round of antiviral medications and then find him an infectious disease doctor. Do you understand all of this?"

"Yes, I do."

I didn't feel the need to mention the organization I had been doing a project for over the last three months. He was a doctor; it was his duty to explain. After taking forty days to tell me what was wrong with my husband, the least he could do was explain. I wasn't angry. I didn't ask where Steven got it. After working at BLCA I had come to learn that once a person was infected, that was all that mattered—do something about it from there. Worrying about the hows wasn't going to help a person get well.

"What else?" I asked. Braced.

"There is a nurse who is also an AIDS counselor for the two of you outside," he said. "She will let you know how you will get tested and what you can do to protect yourself."

I'm thinking, *How am I going to protect myself with my husband? Yeah, send her on in here.*

Steven asked me to stay while he told Uncle Charles and Godmother Martha together. Tears immediately popped into Uncle Charles's eyes, and he wiped them really hard and shook his head as if someone had hit him in it with a bat.

Godmother Martha jumped into nurse mode, quizzing the doctor. "How long do you think he has before he becomes full blown?"

"He's full blown now, his T-cell count is four," answered the doctor. The news of his status rocked her further.

This little meeting was so carefully orchestrated that I bet the doctor and Steven had rehearsed every line. It sounded and felt that way to me.

Uncle Charles and Godmother Martha excused themselves while the nurse came in to speak with us.

"I have to offer you counseling sessions before you can take the HIV test," she said. "This is a Catholic hospital and it is just procedure."

"Miss, you can take my blood right now," I said, rolling up my sleeve. "I don't need any counseling. I've already counseled with the Master Doctor."

Like Bishop Sam says, "The Consultant, whom the consultants consult!"

Steven piped up. "My wife is very religious."

"I'm not *religious*," I corrected him. "I have a personal relationship with Jesus."

"But the counseling is a preparation for what is about to happen now and after," said the nurse convincingly.

"Rabbit, I think you should get the counseling, just in case," Steven said sympathetically.

God walked into the room and sat next to me on the bed. I felt a boldness in Him that was unstoppable.

"Take my blood now so you can tell me I'm negative!" I said confidently. "Since this is a Catholic hospital, I'm sure you believe in Jesus and the power of His Blood. Or do you? I'm covered in it and I'm whole."

"Well, I have to advise my supervisor that you are denying counseling," she said. "And then I'll call you with a date to come in to do it."

"Don't wait forty days like you did to tell me about Steven," I said over-politely. "I deserve the right to take that test ASAP. And if I can't do it here quickly, I'll go somewhere else."

She was so flustered with me! When we all simmered down over the testing issue, she shared some very valuable tips on how to maneuver with a mate with AIDS.

"Are you all having protected sex?" she asked.

"Sometimes yes, sometimes no," Steven answered.

"How often do you have sex?"

"Often," we both answered.

"It is now important to always have protected sex," she urged.

Well, I hope Steven's had enough sex to last him, because

I'm done, I thought. A rubber is not a hundred percent effective. If it can't completely protect you from pregnancy, how can it protect you against AIDS? It's a rubber, and the last time I checked, rubbers leaked.

If this was the type of counseling service the nurse was offering to couples, it was failing miserably. How in the world do you even fix your face to tell a woman to have protected sex with her husband? Who, by the way, has AIDS. I wanted to know who still trusts a condom when you *know* the person has AIDS. Absolutely ludicrous!

"Bleach kills the virus, so always use it when cleaning the bathroom, in the wash, and on dishes."

Steven and I threw each other a knowing look. At the time, I was the bleach-everything-in-the-house queen. If I had to be stuck on a desert island with only one cleaning product, back in those days it would have been bleach.

Miss Nurse promised she'd call me in a week to schedule the test, which she would administer herself.

"If you change your mind about counseling—"

I cut her off. "I need you to respect my position of faith on this one. I'm walking through this fiery trial and through the valley of the shadow of death. I fear no evil, not even AIDS."

She sealed her departure with a hug. She was clear.

Debra picked me up the next day in Brooklyn and drove me to the Gay Men's Health Crisis. They were closed, as it was a Saturday.

"Whaaat! They should never be closed!" she said furiously. "First thing Monday morning you make an appointment with their intake department so you guys can receive the goods and services for PWAs—people with AIDS."

Steven wanted me to have his sisters at the hospital on Sunday so he could tell them one by one. I spent the night at Stacey and Claudette's to tell them as Steven had requested and to be near the hospital. I planned to tell them in the morning, and I was so wound up that I couldn't sleep. I lounged on the couch in their living room and watched TV all night. Stacey got up every other hour to turn off the TV and I'd wave at him to show I wasn't sleeping.

By 7 A.M., I heard him and Claudette discussing my sleepless night, because they have lots of photos of me sleeping soundly at parties. They knew that if I stayed awake for any reason all night, there must be a big problem. I knocked on the door and sat on the edge of their bed.

"I haven't been able to sleep because Steven wanted me to talk to you both, but I didn't know how," I said. "We had a meeting with the doctor and Steven has AIDS."

Stacey grabbed his face and burst into tears. I got off of the bed and held him until he stopped crying. Claudette sat helpless, watching her husband. There was nothing she could do for him. Steven and Stacey had been best friends since they were young kids. When we got to the hospital, Stacey ran into the room and hugged Steven with all of his might. I'm glad he didn't do any more crying, at least not in front of Steven.

Steven wanted Claudette and Stacey to stay in the room while he told his baby sister first, but Stacey excused himself and I knew why. When he told his baby sister, she fell into a fit of tears. When the two of them were together, they were very civil to one another until the older sister arrived on the scene. Then it was definitely girls against boy.

The older sister sat in the chair with her legs crossed, swinging her foot. When he told her, she said, still swinging her foot, "I knew that."

Steven asked, "What do you mean you knew that?"

"Mama knew it and she told me," she said. Following this conversation, I felt like the tennis ball being belted from one side of the net to the other.

My mind flashed back to the wedding video: "You're taking a lot off our hands, chile." "He's your problem now; don't send him back to our house." "See, Steven, I told you about all of that worrying. Everything always works out in the end." Wink, wink.

Nah! And I shook it off.

"Shut up, you're lying, shut up! I hate you!" he screamed at her. Then he went off with his brother-versus-sister tirade: "Ever since we were little . . ."

I couldn't believe that he was going there, in the middle of his death announcement from a hospital bed.

"I hated you then and I hate you now!" he screamed. "Get out of my room!"

She got up calmly and walked out. Claudette and I stared at each other like, "Did that just happen?"

The day of the fire, God said, "Hold on to me and don't let go." That kept flashing through my head like a blinking yellow light.

Now that the immediate family and close friends were informed, the sisters called a meeting to discuss how we would handle this news with the public at large. It was the younger sister who took charge. "We are going to tell everybody that Steven has stomach cancer."

"Why stomach cancer?" I asked.

"Because since he had been in the hospital a lot before for ulcers, it seems normal that he might get stomach cancer," she reasoned.

"Really," I said, unconvinced.

"All right, everyone, are we clear?" she said. "Steven has stomach cancer."

I wished that the declaration of stomach cancer were true; then there would have been no cause for concern over my health. That is a little issue neither of them ever seemed to mention. Even though I knew I wasn't infected. I didn't care if I ever took the test. I knew I was negative, and in that knowing, I had peace.

See, I didn't just start praying when this showed up in my life. I had been God's Girl for a long time. This was a test to see how I could stand in what I'd learned about prayer, to show me that I should relax in my faith. I know God and He definitely knows me. I love how I discover something new about Him each day. One of my favorite songs from Saint John that we used to sing was "Great Is Thy Faithfulness."

It was another full week before Steven was released from the hospital. He had withered down to skin and bones. His six-foot-three frame was all of a hundred and twenty-five pounds. My job was to bring him home and go to work rebuilding him in his own bed and with food from my kitchen.

The first stop he wanted to make was to the office of the attorney we dealt with after the fire. He handled all the legal aspects of Mama Mo's estate. The attorney looked at Steven barely filling up a sweatsuit. It took Steven every ounce of energy he had to walk from the car to the office. He was so totally winded and exhausted by the time he got to the couch that when I sat him down, he toppled over. I sat down next to him and laid his head in my lap while I delivered the news.

The attorney stopped flipping his pen. "I'm so sorry, Steven. How can I help you?"

"I want you to make out my will and leave everything to my wife. I don't want my sisters to get nothing I have," he spat with venom. "One of them killed my mother by leaving that candle burning and they won't say who did it. I hate them for killing my mother!"

"All right," the attorney said, looking at me. He was all too familiar with the family feud.

At one point, right after the fire, Steven wanted to sue his sisters for reckless endangerment or attempted homicide. It was eating him up and he would not let it go. He even went so far as to ask other people what they thought about the idea. Fortunately, they all thought as I did, that it wasn't a good thing to pursue. The problems of those siblings had started long before their house burned down, before their mother died in it, and before Steven got AIDS. However, this latest development in their lives was just another log on the fire to compound their complex relationship.

Steven asked, "How long will it take for you to make out my will? Because I don't know how much longer I have."

"Right away. I can have it in two days," assured the attorney.

It was a laborious process for us to get in the car. Steven may have weighed only a hundred and twenty-five pounds, but it was all dead weight. He had zero strength. He reclined the car seat and fell into a deep sleep as if he'd been working on the railroad all day. Fortunately for him, I had to do the pharmacy and grocery store runs, so he got to sleep for more than two hours before getting home. He needed every minute of it to regain enough strength to get from the car to the bed. Again, another deep sleep for two hours.

Dewanda came over and helped me organize myself. She and her roommate, Lucy, loved them some Steven. During the year we had lived in that brownstone we had lots of activity in our backyard, which was separated from Dewanda and Lucy's by a fence. We used to pass Dewanda's two-year-old daughter over the fence so she could hang out with us as well as share many of our meals.

Lucy kept Steven company while I made dinner. I was grateful for their strong, supportive, and silent company. I didn't have to keep discussing the dilemma over and over with them. They were among the first set of people to whom I divulged the family secret. They were a part of the village I had created for myself since my family was not in New York. One of the first things I was able to accomplish was the assemblage of a group of people that I called family.

His sisters knew he was getting out of the hospital. Where were they on that Friday he came home? Where were they for the rest of the weekend? It was our friends who came to visit, help around the house, and bring good wishes. Karu practically moved in, and he was a beacon of light for us both. We didn't see Steven's sisters at our house for a week. And Steven talked about how sad it made him every day.

I had accepted a full-time position at BLCA as the director of communications, and my start date was the same day I had to take the AIDS test. I got to the hospital early and waited for the nurse outside of her office.

"You're awfully dressed up this morning," she acknowledged.

"I start a new job today at the Black Leadership Commission on AIDS in the city."

She looked at me. "Really?"

"See how God placed me right when I needed to be there?" I said.

The look on her face told me she didn't understand.

"This organization has been around for ten years, and I'd never heard of it until a month before Steven came to the hospital," I explained. "Their office is the headquarters for all of the information and resources a person could want about AIDS for people of color in New York City, and here I was working there at the time of his diagnosis."

"Yes, I see," she said, finally beginning to understand.

I sealed it for her further. "Nobody but Jesus could have executed that plan any better. Just like He's kept me covered in the Blood even though I was having a whole lot of contact with a person with AIDS."

"You sure have a lot of faith," she said.

I rolled up my sleeve and gave her my arm. "Yes, I do. So please hurry and take my blood, I have to get to work."

The director of the BLCA office, Bill, didn't know I had to take my test that morning, so he had called my house looking for me. He said at first he panicked because he thought I had changed my mind. My BLCA family also knew about Steven because they knew AIDS intimately. It was their work, and I was not in the mood to hide this bit of information from the very people who could help us.

Debra had a serious talk with me about personal stuff.

"Are you and Steven kissing?" she asked.

"Not now, 'cause he's got thrush in his mouth," I told her.

"Make sure you don't kiss for a while after he's brushed his teeth. Sometimes a person's gums bleed when brushing. So, if he's infected and you kiss, that can be a point of transmission."

"I haven't read that one."

"You won't," she said. "They can't release that information to the community without really knowing all the details and doing several double-blind studies and all. But it's a body fluid, ain't it?"

"You're right," I said. "Then what about sweat?"

She just pointed to me like, "Yep."

"And tears?"

She raised an eyebrow. I exhaled through my teeth.

This thing was no joke! But these details, while not "written" anywhere, were things any critical thinker could figure out. I received all that on the first day at my new job. Thank you, Lord.

I purposely waited until I took the test to tell my parents about Steven because I didn't want them worried about my status for too long. But I also waited because they were a loving but seriously crazy pair. Sure enough, when I gave them the news, they flipped.

Mommie gasped, "What are you going to do!"

"I'm going to stay here and take care of him," I said.

"I'm coming to get you," Bo Daddy said.

I pleaded, "Come on, y'all. I need you to stick by me and understand my decision. I need y'all to exhibit some of that compassion you taught me to have."

Bo Daddy flipped. "All I'm saying is, you didn't sign up for this. You know you don't have to stay. Pack up!"

"Mommie, please, don't let him come here."

"Honey, hang up the phone!" she said to Bo Daddy, and he hung up, muttering his disapproval.

"What about you?" my mother asked. "Oh, Lord. Are you okay?"

"I took my test this morning," I told her. "I'll have the results in a couple of weeks. And yes, I'm okay and I'm negative."

"How do you know?" she asked.

"God told me so, and I'm standing on the Word you taught me," I reminded her.

"I know, I know," she said. "But listen, remember that burned yellow slip of paper we found after the fire that had Steven's name on it from an HIV test that he said was nothing? I told you we'll see."

Through all of this, I had totally forgotten about that. It had been two years ago. That's what mommies are for, to remind you of life's little things that one day will mean something big.

"I remember now," I said. "I need you to call a family meeting to tell them. His sisters want us to tell everyone that he has stomach cancer. I will tell people who are not a part of our lives that lie because he does deserve to have his privacy protected, but some people have just got to know the truth."

"I think I should wait until you have your test results before I tell everyone else," my mother said.

"Good idea."

"Do you need me to come?"

"Not now," I said, exhaling. "But I will. Mommie, you brought me to Jesus. Remember, He'll never leave us or forsake us. I'm negative, you'll see."

My friend Patti, whose parents are preachers, assembled a group of my mighty prayer warriors for a conference call with people from all over the country who knew of Steven's situation. It included my mother, Lencola, Tyger, Henzy, Bishop Sam, Patti's parents, and friends from L.A. and Atlanta. The objective was to lift up a prayer corporately to expedite his healing. There must have been twenty people on the call. Everyone took turns praying, worshipping, and speaking in tongues. It was totally awesome. I was overcome with the Spirit and at the words lifted to God on our behalf.

Patti was staying the night at our house. I heard her hang up the extension and run to my room when she heard me start to cry. She was a P.K. (preacher's kid), so she knew how to pray, lay hands, and seek the Lord's face.

During the wait for the results, Steven was a new man. He had changed his talk, and judging by the Bible laying next to his nightstand, he was trying to change his walk too.

"I'm so glad we're moving away," he said. "I can't wait to get out of here. Maybe we should go ahead and build that house in the Poconos right now. That way when we get sick, we'll be away from here together—"

"Wait! Wait! Wait!" I said. "Whatever do you mean when *we* get sick?"

"Rabbit, you may not want to deal with the fact that you may be positive, but I have been thinking a lot about it," he said.

"Don't waste your time thinking about that," I warned him. "Don't claim something for me that isn't so!"

"All I'm saying is that one of us needs to look at reality."

"My reality is that God has kept me covered and will continue to cover me," I said. "End of story."

Steven had conjured up these convoluted visions of us getting sick together and then dashing off to some other place to live so we could die together. Now that was a web of deception he was spinning in his own mind.

Two weeks later, the nurse called me to her office for the results. I was annoyed at how she was delaying telling me I was negative, but I let her have her moment.

"Your results came back negative," she said, beaming.

"Thank you, Jesus!" I praised.

"I have learned to have more faith because of you," she testified. "We all actually thought there would be two cases of AIDS here, but you were so sure you were negative. I've been a nervous wreck waiting for these results to come back and you didn't even seem worried."

"No, I wasn't worried, because if you're going to pray, why worry, and if you're going to worry, why pray?" I said. "There really was no need to waste one night's sleep over it. Well, I did lose one night's sleep when I had to tell Steven's best friend, but that's it."

I could tell that this woman was religious. She had all of the artifacts a lot of Catholics have around that let you know they're Catholic. This nurse was a woman of faith, but she failed to bring her faith to work. She hadn't yet activated her faith into full operation, because if she had, she'd never have been able to separate it from herself. Also, she wouldn't have been so surprised to see faith at work in someone who knew how to activate it. I understood very clearly that it was my faith that had made me whole.

God's hand was holding me through this test. I've learned to discern the hand of God by coming out of what could have destroyed me.

CHAPTER FIVE

The Caregiving

But be ye doers of the word, and not hearers only,
deceiving your own selves.

For if any be a hearer of the word, and not a doer,
he is like unto a man beholding his natural face in a glass:
For he beholds himself, and goes his way, and straightway
forgets what manner of a man he was.

But whoso looks into the perfect law of liberty, and
continues therein, he being not a forgetful hearer, but a
doer of the work, this man will be blessed in his deed.

—JAMES 1:22–25

From the moment I told Steven I was negative, he went back to his Jekyll and Hyde routine. At first, I couldn't understand why he was so ornery. I made sure that I did not flaunt my negative status around him, but as my peace increased, so did his meanness. Ruthie was Steven's full-time caregiver during the day while I worked at BLCA. She had been a nurse's aide at one time and she knew all about taking care of sick people. Retnuh Relations needed to add another department, the Florence Nightingale division.

As directed by Debra, we went to the Gay Men's Health Crisis (GMHC) for our intake appointment so Steven could be registered for goods and services. They had a flight of stairs to the counselor's office, and after Steven climbed them, he had to lay down, as always with his head in my lap. He was so exhausted he could barely answer the questions.

"How do you think you contracted the virus?" asked the counselor.

"I don't even know. I'm not sure," he answered shakily.

"Steven was married before and his wife was a drug abuser who had relations with other men," I offered. Steven had never even considered that until I said it.

The counselor reluctantly agreed, "That's a real possibility."

The statement was not finite; it had a hint of "But what else is there?" waving in the air.

"Is your ex-wife infected?" the counselor logically asked.

Steven seemed wary of the line of questioning. "I haven't spoken to her, so I honestly don't know."

GMHC loaded us down with information, Ensure drinks to help boost his weight, and loads of rubbers. There was an appointment made for a nutritionist to come to our apartment so that Steven could get on the road to gaining weight and getting his strength back.

I began making the Ensure drinks in various ways so that he could get them down without being bored. I'd mix the chocolate and strawberry flavors with crushed ice like a milkshake. I'd heat the chocolate flavor and serve it like hot chocolate, and the vanilla I would freeze really cold and serve it with breakfast like milk.

I knew that the AIDS medication was supposed to decrease his viral load, but it was destroying everything else in its path. I made teas with immune-building properties, like dandelion, red clover, alfalfa, goldenseal, and echinacea. He hated drinking them, so I'd stand over him with an Ensure treat to drink right behind it. Twice a day I'd also make him a smoothie with spirulina, chlorophyll, bluegreen algae, barley, wheatgrass, and flaxseed. I'd blend it with frozen fruits, like strawberries, apples, and bananas, in fruit juices.

It was mandatory that he drink a cup of aloe vera water every hour he was awake. The water was to keep his elimination tract open and to run the toxins from the medication out of his body. I made the aloe water by freezing the plant, then cutting the frozen pieces and placing them in water containers like ice cubes. He complained that it was bitter and it had him running to the bathroom too much.

"When you get to the point where you can literally run to the bathroom, you can stop drinking so much," I told him.

My methodology was also an effort to get him out of that bed and away from the television for some exercise. Any person who lay in a bed for forty-plus days, hooked up to a catheter, seriously needed exercise.

Every other day, I'd dry-brush his entire body and put him in the Jacuzzi tub for a Dead Sea salt soak. The dry-brushing helped to slough off the dead skin and to stimulate the circulation, and the Dead Sea salts would draw toxins from the body that were ready to be eliminated but needed a little help.

His face had broken out terribly, a reaction from all of those medications in his system, undoubtedly. So every night I gave him an egg-white facial, since his skin was oily. He'd relax with the facial on while sipping his green smoothie through a straw. When the egg mask had hardened, I used warm towels to melt the mask and then wipe it off. He loved this ritual and his face started to clear.

I created meals high in carbohydrates and protein. Every meat dish had mashed potatoes with gravy, or a baked potato with real butter, or brown or basmati rice with gravy. We always had my garbage salad first—it could have been a meal all by itself—and at least one fresh cooked vegetable like green beans, collard or turnip greens, beets, turnips, or cabbage.

I had a bread maker and it seemed to never stop churning out loaves. At every meal, three times a day, he was served a chunk of homemade bread toasted warm, with butter. Depending on the meal, I'd whip up some sweet corn bread or hot-water corn bread for a diversion. Once weekly, we had a pot of lima beans, great northern beans, lentils, or red beans and brown rice as the main event. Steven was in hog heaven. Like my Grannie would say, "Make sure you keep a pot on your stove."

"Rabbit, these meals are so good, but can a brother get a pork chop?" he would ask, knowing the answer already.

"Absolutely not! No pork chops, no pork bacon, no pigs' feet, no oxtails!" I admonished. "I'll make you a deal:

when you feel well enough to drive yourself to the store and buy the pork chops yourself, I'll fry them up real crispy just the way you like them."

"Deal!" he said with a mouth full of bread.

At his next doctor's visit he had gained a full ten pounds in the fifteen days he'd been out of the hospital. The doctor was amazed with his at-home recovery. When he asked me what I was doing, he couldn't wrap his head around it all. He didn't at all agree with the herbal stuff, but he admitted he didn't fully understand it either.

"With all due respect, Doctor," said Steven, a little peeved, "I was in the hospital here all of those weeks and I kept feeling worse and worse. The food sucked, the beds were hard, and you were pumping me with all this medicine. Whatever the wife is doing for me, I'm going to keep doing it, because I really feel better. Not great, but better."

Well, well, well, I thought. Since our health regimen showed steady improvements in Steven, we faithfully kept it going.

By Christmas, he was able to walk around the house and go up and down the stairs in our duplex with little effort. When my parents came for Christmas, I bought them Broadway show tickets.

Steven had chosen to take up the art of selective prudence. He argued with me about the ticket purchase in front of my parents. He also got in my face and ordered me not to move the car to drive them to the theater, which was appropriately parked for the next day's alternate-side-of-the-street parking. He was so busy getting in my face, arguing and fussing on the narrow staircase, that he fell backward down the steps for no apparent reason.

"I keep telling you to quit fooling with me, I'm God's Girl for real," I chastised him. "You'll figure it out."

I marched out of the house with my parents in tow, got in the car, and drove them to the city. My parents were fuming.

"That boy done gone stark raving mad!" Bo Daddy assessed. "You need to get away from that fool."

Mommie sucked her teeth. "Huh, I don't know how you deal with him, myself. He's always huffing and barking at you. I don't care what's wrong with him, he has no business trying to get all in your face like that, LaJoyce."

This was the worst possible thing for my parents to see. It was also the worst thing for Steven to pull for the first time. This wasn't his family he was trying to get bad in front of, it was mine. Did he actually think that my parents were going to cosign his anger over moving the car?

Parking in our neighborhood was tight, but I found that if you said a little prayer right before turning the corner, there would be a space waiting for you or someone would pull out just in time. Steven called me nutty to think that way, but it always worked while I was driving. Now that he was sick, he got to see it work more and more.

We started off the new year right, with Bishop Sam hosting Bible study at our house. We had our regular attendees, Lencola, Arlene (my girl from college), my client Dr. Pepsi, Clive, and Ruthie. We had a loveseat, and the left corner was designated the "crying corner." It never failed, because whoever sat in that corner had some kind of breakthrough or a tearful testimony every week. Bishop Sam always had incredible lessons and Steven respected him the most over any other man of the cloth.

By February 1993, Steven had gained his weight back and was working again. To look at him, you would never have thought he had full-blown AIDS. The doctors were all confounded by his miraculous recovery. They had not told us, but they didn't think he would live two weeks after leaving the hospital.

I was so burned out from taking care of Steven that I resigned from my post as director of communications at BLCA. It was just too much for me to do AIDS at home and at work. The emotional strain was starting to tax me. I knew I had to bail out before I suffered a nervous breakdown. I wasn't frail to the point of having one, but I felt it was coming if I didn't make some changes.

My client roster with Retnuh Relations was in full swing, with clients like E. Lynn Harris; *Billboard* magazine's pre-Grammy party; and dreamologist Dr. Pepsi.

I had to coordinate the *Billboard* pre-Grammy party for the industry people. The manager of the *Billboard* R&B chart, Terri Rossi, was an industry luminary and my mentor. We landed a major coup by garnering the attendance of Aretha Franklin and James Brown. The attendee list was the who's-who of the business, as well as the artists to be awarded.

The party was a formal affair, so Steven and I wore

matching Franklin Rowe outfits. The party was for one thousand very VIPs, and security had to be tight. For the first time, I needed to get Steven involved in an event. Since he liked playing policeman, I put him in charge of security. He called his group the Lakeview Connection because he went back to his Long Island neighborhood and got twenty people from his crew to stand watch. On that night he was the party police. Steven, Stacey, Claudette, and the others were a superb crew and Steven had coordinated it all.

In other business, E. Lynn Harris had been a friend of mine since the early 1980s. He, like Lencola, is from Arkansas. Lynn always said he dreamed of a career as an author, and I volunteered to help him when he self-published a novel called *Invisible Life*.

Steven could not stand Lynn. I mean, he downright hated him. Every time I mentioned his name, Steven would say, "Don't mention that faggot's name in front of me!"

If Lynn would call, Steven would say, "Tell that faggot not to call here when I'm home!" He'd make sure he said it loud enough for Lynn to hear.

"How can you call yourself a Christian and have gay friends!" he would say to me.

No, he didn't have the nerve to go there.

Steven totally embarrassed me when he cussed Lynn out on the phone for utilizing our FedEx number, which I said he could use. Steven demanded he send us money ASAP and told him to never use our account again. Lynn was just getting started back then, so hey, if I could share my FedEx number with him to send a few books around, why not?

I'd had enough of Steven.

"You may not like my gay friends, but they were here for me in this city long before you came along," I told him. "Lynn and I have been through more together than you and I will get to go through for a lifetime. We're friends forever! So get over it!"

I never mentioned him again to Steven. To this day, Lynn and I are still friends.

Steven and I started taking weekend trips to the Poconos again, in search of the right builder for our home. We had met a wonderful sister in our new community named Ellen who opened her home to us on weekends until we were situated. Once we decided on a builder, we found a house to rent nearby until ours was ready—for only seven hundred dollars. That was going to be a huge savings for us. Claudette and Stacey also planned to make the move to their chalet and we decided we'd all do it together.

A couple of weeks before we were to move, Steven was shopping his brains out. He went to Saks Fifth Avenue and purchased an eleven-hundred-dollar suit! This man was spending money like he was going to die next week. He didn't want there to be anything left over for anyone to get.

"You're kidding, right?" I asked him. "You don't come home to show your wife some suit you just bought at Saks for eleven hundred dollars and expect her to be okay with it! Unless you're Donald Trump. Take it back!"

"I deserve this suit," he said, trying to convince me.

"Do you know how many herbs we can buy to keep you well with that money? That's a month and a half's rent on the rental house, or the mortgage payment on our new home. Take it back!"

"You can forget that, because after all I've been through, I deserve this new suit," he lamented.

I tried another angle. "If Franklin can make this suit identically, will you take it back?"

He eyed the suit. "Franklin can't make stuff this well, it came from Saks," he said.

I threw my hands up. Duke's advice resounded in my head: don't be logical with illogical people.

Steven decided he wasn't going to speak to me, for whatever reason. And he chose to sleep on the couch in the office. This went on for two weeks. Every time I tried to talk to him, he'd say to me, "I'm not talking to you. I don't hear you."

Was this a marriage or grade school?

"It's been more than a week since you haven't spoken to me," I said. "How long do you think you can live in the same house without speaking to someone?"

He finally had a real answer. "I didn't speak to my sister once for three months."

"Well, I ain't your sister," I said. "So if you don't want to respect me as your wife, I won't be one."

I went on strike. I stopped washing his clothes and

cooking, and I didn't bother to clean the office where he chose to sleep. When it got to the point where we needed to talk about things regarding our move and he didn't want to, I started collecting boxes for my own things.

My Chicago buddy Terria, transplanted to New York like me, came over during our silent feud. Steven was having a nonverbal tantrum, stomping up and down the stairs, slamming doors, throwing things around. He was always selective about to whom he would show his true colors, and Terria was a frequent recipient. She and I were lounging on my bed, talking, when I asked her to pass my purse.

"Girlie, I don't know how you stay here with him, when he's so mean to you," she said. Her arm dropped at the unexpected weight of my bag. "What in the world do you have in there?"

"You know what they say about us Chicago women?" I said. "We come packing!"

I told her of the old Chi-town folklore as I let her get a peek at my gun.

Terria was totally shocked. "Why do you have that?!"

"Just in case Steven wants to find out what being from the South Side of Chicago really means," I said. "Let him keep acting crazy with me, and AIDS won't be what kills him."

Years later, Terria confided that this experience left her traumatized, and for my actions I truly apologize.

I packed my dishes, records, and clothes and called Dewanda over to disconnect my computer. She cried the whole time. Then I called two friends: Ellen, to drive me to the Poconos, and Garfield, to help load boxes for the move.

Steven screamed at me for moving the computer.

"I bought that computer with my mother's money," he whined. "You leave it here. It's mine!"

I quietly left the box and came back with five thousand dollars in cash, placed it on the table in front of him, and packed up the computer. While he was running all over town spending his money, I was saving mine.

I wanted to move on a Wednesday during the day while Steven was at work, but Garfield called to say that he was in the Bahamas and asked if I could wait until he returned on Friday. Ellen came straight to Brooklyn in her truck with boxes so we could roll out.

"I had a talk with Steven," she said as I folded my clothes and put them in boxes.

"Oh yeah, Steven? You mean he speaks?" I said as she laughed.

"He told me everything," she said somberly, sitting on the bed.

"Everything?" I quizzed with a raised eyebrow.

"Yes, everything."

I went in for the jugular. "Did he tell you he has AIDS?"

When she gasped, I knew he hadn't told her that little detail.

"No, he didn't tell me that, but he did tell me how much he loves you and that he doesn't want you to go."

"Then he can tell me himself," I said, unfazed.

In the wee hours of the morning on my moving day, I

felt the covers snatched off of me, and Steven climbed
into bed crying hysterically for me not to leave. Part of his
behavior was also due to him not wanting to move to the
Poconos after all.

"Steven, you can live wherever you want," I told him.
"LaJoyce is moving to the Poconos."

"Then I guess we're moving together. I love you too
much to let you go," he pleaded.

"I do love you, but not at the expense of my emotional
health. I can turn it off or on just like that," I said with a
snap. "I told you to quit trying me, I ain't your sisters. I'm
your wife and you should treat me with more respect than
you have."

"I'm sorry."

"How many women do you know who would have
stayed around once they got the news about your condition?" I asked. "I need you to be clear that wanting to move
out had nothing to do with your diagnosis, but everything
to do with your attitude."

"I'll do better," he promised.

"Okay, then. I'll tell Ellen I'm not going."

At Bible study that evening, Steven told everyone, "I
almost didn't come up here tonight, but I didn't let the
devil win."

Everyone shouted their hallelujah praises for Steven's
about-face. There sat my closest friends, and they all knew
the deal.

We moved into our rental house over the Fourth of
July weekend, and it was 107 degrees in the shade of the
Pocono Mountains! I organized the house posthaste be-

cause I had to take a road trip the following weekend to my college campus, Eastern Illinois University in Charleston, Illinois, for our Black Student Reunion. My former roomie, Angela, and I did a presentation called "AIDS 101: Issues for People of Color." Angela was a serious sister who was an AIDS educator for the Department of Health, training the Chicago Police Department on every facet of AIDS.

We marveled at how we had both come across this line of work helping others through this crisis. She and I rented a car to drive to Chicago after the reunion and while she slept, I cried like a baby up Interstate 57 North, toiling about how I should tell her that the AIDS epidemic had hit my home as well. Angela and I shared the deepest of secrets, as college roomies do. This was something so close to us both, closer than she had ever imagined.

I decided that for one weekend, I'd be free of such cumbersome conversation. I wanted for a moment to enjoy my friend and my freedom. I didn't want to shed any tears, to give any backstories, or to get any sympathy. I was totally the LaJoyce that Angela remembered. She and I had vowed we'd be friends for life. I didn't want her to know that life had shown up front and center in the form of AIDS.

When I returned home from that trip Steven announced, "I'm buying a dog today and I don't care what you say."

"Why has it got to be all like that?" I said. "I love dogs. See there, you're expecting a positive thing to be a negative. Stop it!"

The most adorable white German shepherd puppy

came to live with us. I named her Missy in honor of the German shepherd Grannie once owned. Missy immediately became my dog. This drove Steven to purchase a dog "just for me," he said—a Rottweiler we named Rambo.

Soon after we moved to the Poconos and broke ground on our home, Steven was downsized and lost his job as the assistant parts manager for the BMW dealership where he worked. It was only about two weeks before he got another position at a luxury parts sales company in central New Jersey. I had gone to work for Patti at her public relations company in Somerville, New Jersey, and we began carpooling, with him dropping me off first.

It was just in the nick of time that Steven didn't have to go to the city anymore. His temperament was unable to handle the New York City traffic any longer. It seemed as though every day, he'd have a road rage experience. In one episode on the way to Queens to visit Uncle Charles, a guy in another car literally scraped my side of the car during Steven's tirade. At the next light, I got out in the middle of the street and took the subway.

Steven had been preoccupied with death ever since his diagnosis. He said he always felt that he wouldn't live to be thirty-three years old. It was a result of some freaky recurring dream he had, so he said.

The night before his thirty-third birthday, he refused to go to sleep. I promised him I'd stay awake, but true to form I fell asleep at nine thirty. I awoke at four in the morning and found him sleeping. I shook him awake to let him know he was still breathing. He was so happy, and I for him, that we had sex—with a rubber—right then.

He was constantly exhibiting classic death-wish behavior. So his acting out with his car and in other places let me know that although he was blessed to still be in the game of life, he did not know how to play it. For the way to play the game of life is with God before you.

We moved into our newly built home on my birthday weekend of September 1994. But not before our pastor, K.P., came to pray in every room before any furniture went in it. I had been introduced to his church by Ellen; I never missed a Tuesday night Bible study and my boldness in the Lord increased even more under this ministry. Steven liked to attend occasionally on Sundays. What we enjoyed most was fellowship with our prophetic, anointed, and crazy new pastor, K.P.

Steven had taken ill after the Saturday portion of the move with our local friends. On Sunday, I had to do all of the moving with the friends who had come to lend a hand. In my opinion, Steven was running a game on me by saying he was so ill that he couldn't help. He didn't like the crew I had called in—three of my gay friends.

"Why you gotta call them? You know how I feel. I just want to do the move and get it over with. I hope they aren't spending the night! I don't want them in my house overnight," he shouted angrily.

He didn't want them in his house overnight now, but it was okay when we'd had the three of them up with Dewanda and Lucy one weekend. The gay crew took over and did all of the cooking and brought all of the food for the mountain festivities. Dewanda remembered later that Steven took Missy, left us at home, and was gone until nightfall. He said he'd gone to our property for the new house and he got lost in the woods. Dewanda said it sounded strange to her then, but she never said anything at the time.

So he chose to play the avoidance game, pretending to be sick on the final day of our move. I had to ask God's forgiveness on that one, for real. My anger was creeping dangerously in Steven's direction with all of the crap he was pulling. Without the AIDS diagnosis, his behavior was enough to make anyone want to pop him in the face on a regular basis. Now compound that with AIDS, and it was a potentially lethal combination.

Steven was coming down with bouts of dementia. Sometimes he was totally lucid, and other times he was as nutty as a fruitcake. Because of his preexisting health condition, we couldn't obtain any additional life insurance on him. I signed up for credit life insurance on the house, but that just covered me. For my physical exam for the credit life insurance, the insurance company sent a nurse to our home and I had to present photo identification. Steven wanted to ask Stacey to pose as him so that we'd both be able to get credit life.

"Honey, that's insurance fraud!" I told him.

"But you are not going to get much insurance money," he said. "At least the house will be paid off when I die. I'll ask Stacey, he will do it for me."

"How can you go to sleep at night conjuring up such a mess?" I said. "It's not fair for you to ask your best friend to commit insurance fraud for you."

"I guess you're right."

"You better not ask him, Steven."

"Okay, okay. I won't," he conceded.

Years later, when we were discussing this, Stacey and Claudette exchanged glances knowingly, because Steven called him after all behind my back and asked him to commit the crime. I thought, *Some best friend, huh?*

Fortunately, I had my work to keep me busy. Patti had an awesome client roster with Stephanie Mills, George Howard, LeVert, and the O'Jays. Patti turned George Howard over to me, because he had been a thorn in the side of GRP Records when it came to the press. My job: mend old broken relationships with media outlets, and get George to see he was a star.

I threw everything I had into George, including the kitchen sink, taking him fresh-baked goodies on our first meeting. I started calling him GH after that and he became a media darling nationwide. We hit it off so well that we ended up calling one another brother and sister. Then at a family gathering, we discovered we *were* related—very, very distantly, but related nonetheless. Not only was he a relative but he also became my best friend, next to Tyger, that is. I even tried to hook them up when he got divorced! But that's another book.

Steven loved George Howard's jazzy saxophone music and he played it all of the time on the shows he produced for Vaughn Harper. Because he liked GH's music so much, he was tolerant of my going into the city to be with GH or travel with him on road trips.

One day in October 1994, right in the middle of our workday, Steven appeared at the office door, propping himself up on it.

"Rabbit, I'm sick," he managed to say. "You gotta take me to the hospital."

All conversations ceased. Patti hung up the phone mid-conversation and put her shoes on; I followed suit. We had to help him down the stairs. He had just driven me there less than three hours before. *How did he get so sick so fast?*

With the condition he was in, and considering our distance from the Poconos, we needed to get to an emergency room.

Patti drove us to JFK Medical Center in nearby Edison, New Jersey, where Steven was placed in a sterile room. He was diagnosed with PCP—again. Upon entering his room, you had to don a gown, gloves, head and shoe coverings, and a face mask. There was absolutely no spending the night in there. It was treated like an intensive care unit but with private rooms.

I spent many nights on the couch in the living room at Patti's house during the week, so I could already be at work. Her family was wonderful in extending their hospitality to me while I balanced Steven, work, and my Pocono household. I had hired teenagers, Jelani and Gyasi, as dog walkers for Missy and Rambo during the week. I went home on Wednesdays and Fridays. Steven stayed at JFK for a month.

His doctor advised that Steven was going to be officially put on permanent disability. *Wow, I have a disabled husband,* I thought. It was easier to deal with when he was feeling good and not looking sick. I had to start my Florence Nightingale role all over again. I knew what to do. I'd done this all before and he'd gotten well.

God said, "Hold on and don't let go."

What I didn't know how to manage was my mounting emotional stress and the system that we were being thrown into. When I went to Social Services to apply for food stamps, the caseworker said that Steven had to apply in person.

"But, miss, he can't sit up in a car. Do you make house calls?" I wanted to know.

"You have to bring him here and I have to see that he is alive and a real person. I'm sorry, but people have abused the system to the point that this is how we have to do it now."

I made an appointment for two days later and then laid Steven down on a pallet in the truck and drove to the next town so the lady could see him. Her face was ashen when she looked at this sick shell of a man who was just thirty-three years old. She gave me a sympathetic look. I hated it when people looked at me like that. It was my new reality and I needed to deal with it.

Meanwhile, we were sinking financially. As much as I liked working with Patti, I needed to find another job. I made sure I paid the mortgage first and did a juggling act to keep everything else in the air. I had us on payment plans with everyone from the man who delivered the wood to the phone company. Steven discussed bankruptcy for himself, but first he wanted to charge his credit cards up to the hilt. I didn't like that idea at all.

The next day, the lady from Social Services called to say we were denied food stamps because Steven's disability check from New Jersey was one hundred dollars too much. I understood why people cheated the system. When you needed it most, nothing was there. I needed another job, fast.

My parents came for Christmas, along with my brother Stevie, and his son, Cory. It was their first time seeing the new house. My mother was totally into decorating the windows and decking the halls with boughs of holly.

Steven loved Christmas but he was battling a slight fever for a couple of days. Fevers were the measuring point of infection. He refused to take the infection medication and asked me to whip up an herbal remedy instead. I felt we should go to the hospital, because he was still cold with the heat on ninety and several comforters. I knew the last thing he wanted to do was go to the hospital on Christmas Eve, but I was willing if it was necessary. Fortunately, his temperature only went up to a hundred that night and he slept well.

On Christmas morning, I heard the headboard banging in my bedroom. I ran upstairs to look, and from the doorway I shouted downstairs, "Call nine-one-one! Steven is having a seizure!"

I grabbed his hands so he wouldn't hurt himself.

In our community, we had an internal paramedic unit

that was dispatched within minutes of a 911 call. Mr. Frailey, our neighbor, was at the door in five minutes, arriving just after Steven's second seizure. Mr. Frailey was retired from the Pocono Medical Center and it was rumored that he was most awesome. I witnessed it firsthand when he put his fingers on Steven's cheek and belted out, "One oh four point five!"

When the paramedics from town got there, sure enough the fever was 104.5. *He's my own personal angel right here,* I thought of Mr. Frailey. I stepped into the hall to speak with the paramedics and Steven began seizing again, number three. After he was stabilized, it was clear they needed to strap him to a gurney and get to the hospital. I was crying a steady stream of tears. My mother held my hand. Just as the paramedics got to the door with him, he had another seizure, number four.

Bo Daddy and I followed the ambulance to the Pocono Medical Center. Steven was admitted on Christmas Day. Wasn't it just like Jesus to arrange His special day so that you could show His love by taking care of someone else?

Steven was in a catatonic state. He had a collapsed lung as a result of the recent pneumonia, and all of that seizing also contributed.

"It will be a miracle if he makes it through the next forty-eight hours," the doctors said.

I wanted Steven to hold on. There were things that I knew he needed to get right with his sisters before he checked out of here. We stayed in his room awhile, but he was barely there. The doctors said that was a side effect of so many consecutive grand mal seizures accompanied by a high fever. There was nothing we could do but wait it out, and it was best to do that at home.

Two days later, Steven snapped out of his catatonic state enough to give me specific instructions.

"I'm thinking about going bankrupt for real now," he said. "I want you to go and run up the credit cards. Get everything we want."

"Seriously?" I didn't have time to do such a thing, nor did I think it was right.

He started making a list. "Take Mommie shopping, because she's been here through all of my crises, and Bo, too."

Bo Daddy piped up. "Nah, we don't need nothing."

"Make sure you do something good for Fabia; I'm so proud of her."

Fabia was Uncle Charles's daughter, who was an undergrad at Colgate University on a scholarship and headed to law school at Villanova, again on a scholarship. We were all proud of our Fabia. As Steven sat there making out his wish list, I have to admit I got caught up in the excitement. I hadn't bought myself anything in quite some time.

I wasn't much of a shopper because growing up, my mother took us shopping with her every day. *Every* day. To this day, shopping is not a pleasure, it's a necessity.

"Steven, are you sure?" I asked again.

"Do it," he said.

"Okay, I'll start tomorrow."

CHAPTER SIX

The Realization of the Truth

And ye shall know the truth, and the truth shall make you free.

—JOHN 8:32

My little brother Stevie, my nephew Cory, and I hit the malls early and stayed there all day. I was not at all comfortable. It was very hard for me to spend money like that. There was no joy in it, but it was definitely a fever that we all got caught up in. When I ran out of ideas for things to buy, I'd just walk into a store and ask for a few hundred dollars' worth of gift certificates. I couldn't believe I didn't really know what to buy.

Stevie got stuff to fix up the basement. That would be one thing Steven would love when he got home. When his sisters came, they were presented with very lovely things as well as gift certificates. As promised, Fabia was also taken shopping.

A very interesting thing happened on the second day of the shopping spree: the number twenty-four kept appearing everywhere. It was twenty-four past the hour every time I looked. The counter on the tape player would be on twenty-four. The change I had to pay at the store would be twenty-four cents. The change I would receive would be twenty-four cents. That number had always been significant for me because it is the date of my birthday. At first I thought that's all it was—just a number I had an affinity toward because I was born on the twenty-fourth. And so I kept seeing it, perhaps because I was looking for it.

But I remembered a preacher somewhere saying that if you keep seeing a number, it doesn't mean for you to run out and play that number. It means for you to look up that psalm, because there is a message for you. I made a mental note to read Psalm 24 when I got home.

We visited Steven, who was sleeping soundly by the time we got to the hospital, and I woke him to let him know I was there. The first thing he wanted to know was, did I go shopping? I nodded.

"Good," he said, turning his head. "Go home, Rabbit, and get some sleep."

I followed his instruction; I was exhausted from all of that shopping.

I told my mother and Bo Daddy that I was going to take a bath and go to sleep. Just as I crawled into the bed and was about to turn off the TV, the doctor called to say I needed to come back to the hospital right away to sign papers for Steven to get a blood transfusion or he wouldn't make it through the night.

"I'm on my way," I said. "Lord, what is all of this?"

Just as I was going to turn off the TV to get dressed, I

hit the Time button on the remote instead. It read 10:24! That reminded me to read Psalm 24. I grabbed my Bible—it would only take a minute:

> The earth is the Lord's, and the fullness thereof; the world, and they that dwell therein.
> For he hath founded it upon the seas, and established it upon the floods.
> Who shall ascend into the hill of the Lord? Or who shall stand in his holy place?
> He that hath clean hands, and a pure heart; who hath not lifted up his soul unto vanity, nor sworn deceitfully.
> He shall receive the blessing from the Lord, and righteousness from the God of his salvation.
> This is the generation of them that seek him, that seek thy face, O Jacob. Selah.
> Lift up your heads, O ye gates; and be ye lifted up, ye everlasting doors; and the King of glory shall come in.
> Who is this King of glory? The Lord strong and mighty, the Lord mighty in battle.
> Lift up your heads, O ye gates; even lifted them up, ye everlasting doors; and the King of glory shall come in.
> Who is this King of glory? The Lord of hosts, he is the King of glory. Selah.

I closed the Bible to get up to leave and the Spirit said, "Wait a minute! Meditate on that."

I remembered singing the song "Lift Up Your Heads, O Ye Gates" in the children's choir. The music flooded my memory. Then I opened the Bible again and my eyes fell on:

> Who shall ascend into the hill of the Lord? Or who
> shall stand in his holy place?

Then it hit me: this was about Steven. The Scripture asks this with a question mark. He was the only one, at that moment, whom I knew would soon make his ascent into the hill of the Lord and stand in his holy place. The Scripture went on to answer the very question it asked. And the answer was:

> He that hath clean hands, and a pure heart . . .

"Isn't Steven's heart pure? Aren't his hands clean?" I asked myself aloud.

The Holy Spirit told me, "Get the medical records." I reached into the bottom of Steven's nightstand for the four hundred dollars' worth of medical records from Mercy Hospital. I started from the back, not knowing what I was searching for.

The Holy Spirit told me, "Start from the beginning."

It was there that I saw it. On the very first day Steven had gone to Mercy Hospital, it was written, "Patient confirms he has HIV."

My body went numb. "Hold up!" I said out loud, "hold up!"

I read those handwritten words again. They knew from the first day he went to the hospital? A million questions ran through my mind.

Why didn't they tell me on day one? Why would they make me wait forty days?! How could a doctor not tell a wife that her own husband had AIDS?

I answered that last one on my own: policy.

I read the handwritten words again and then I saw even more clearly the words "patient confirms."

That means Steven *told* them he had AIDS. That means he knew! He knew *all along* that he had HIV. I was dumbfounded. I just sat staring at the blank white wall in my room. Then right before my eyes, God replayed for me everything He had tried to show me but I had refused to see.

It started with the first day I met him, when Steven said he was in the hospital for bleeding ulcers. That was lie number one. He didn't even know me a half hour before he started lying to me. He knew he had HIV and chose to have unprotected sex with me! He could have let *me* choose. He took away my freedom of choice in making the decision to be with him or not in spite of his disease.

This also meant he didn't do this by himself, he had help in his mother. The movie continued to play . . .

Mama Mo saying, "Don't wait on money to get married." And "I'll send you on a honeymoon for fifteen days." And asking my parents for money because "you'll never get this opportunity again to go to Hawaii." And paying for an abortion.

Well, I'll be doggone! Since they were choosing to be

in denial about Steven having AIDS, they were also uned-
ucated about the disease to the point that when I got pregnant, they thought there would also be an AIDS-infected
baby, not knowing that if the mother is negative, then the
baby is absolutely negative.

So now they've got the blood of an innocent baby on
their hands. I hope Mama Mo asked for forgiveness from
God like I did. Her motivation seemed entirely different
than mine. For Mama Mo and Steven, the abortion was all
in the name of this secret they were harboring. A deadly
secret.

The movie on the wall played the wedding:

Me before: "I've got the strangest feeling I shouldn't
be doing this."

The older sister: "You just don't know, you're taking a
lot off our hands, chile!"

The younger sister: "He's your problem now; don't
send him back to our house!"

Mama Mo: "See, Steven, I told you about all of that
worrying. Everything always works out in the end." (Wink,
wink.)

"Whaaaaat!" I said, crying. "They *all* knew! Everyone
knew but me?"

Eleven months of dating, two years of marriage, and
lots of sex—funny, he never mentioned it.

The movie kept playing . . .

Steven spending money like a man who would never
have any more. Steven wanting to take a bath before going
to the hospital, because he thought he wasn't coming back.

His older sister saying she knew he had AIDS when he made the announcement. Steven being sure that I was sick, too. Steven not being sure where he got the disease— or deeper yet, not willing to *admit* where he got the disease. All of the disappearing acts he pulled over the years played out. And finally the night of the fire when he fell to his knees asking, "Who am I going to tell all my secrets to now?"

I was numb as I sat on the edge of my bed digesting all this. One thing was for sure: there was *no* way I was going to go down to that hospital to sign any papers for a blood transfusion. He'd just have to die before morning.

I started talking to God. "Help me make some sense of this?"

God had already shown me what He had been trying to tell me. But no, I was so busy worrying about not having a husband at age twenty-eight, and planning my wedding, that I refused to see things put right in my face. I also was in direct violation of the Word by going out to find a "good man."

The Bible is very clear in Proverbs 18:22. It says:

"He who finds a wife, findeth a good thing."

It does **not** say *she* who finds a *man* finds a good thing.

I had to praise the Lord for keeping me through all of my stupidity. I was just like the little kid who kept saying, "Daddy please, Daddy please." Until finally Daddy just said, "Here!"

I repented for being disobedient. I know that delayed obedience is disobedience.

"Lord, right now I have the power of Steven's life in my hands," I said.

I could have very easily lain down, fallen asleep, and conveniently forgotten about going to the hospital. I could have run to show everyone the medical records that had the documentation of what he had done. I could have taken that piece of evidence to the police and had him arrested for attempted murder. And I could have taken the wedding video to the police also and brought both sisters up on the same charges, and added conspiracy to boot. Or I could have just shown the medical records to my brother downstairs and he'd have called for reinforcements from my other brothers in Chicago, and they'd have been here by morning. Not a pretty sight.

"What am I going to get, Lord, if I do the right thing here and now?" I pleaded. "I need you to tell me, how am I going to benefit from, once again, taking the high road? For once I'm asking, what are you going to do for LaJoyce? And please don't take all night to answer me. I need to know right now. Or tonight, Steven is a dead man."

God had never been more clear to me than at that very moment.

Vengeance is mine. I've got this. Stand still and I will bless you. Don't tell anyone tonight about your discovery. Leave now.

I wiped my face, put on clothes, went downstairs, and asked Bo Daddy to ride with me. I signed the papers at the hospital. They said they thought I wasn't coming. The doctor was just about to call me again when I arrived. I didn't want to go into Steven's room. I didn't want to see him. I just signed and left.

Back in my room, I thanked God for His promise and I wholeheartedly forgave Steven. He had to have been a fool for trying to do in a child of the King. I needed to forgive him because he had no clue that I was God's Girl—for real!

I thanked God for keeping me. Quite simply, it was nothing but the Blood of Jesus keeping me covered, with a negative HIV status and safe from harm and danger. I sang myself to sleep with "When You Walk Through a Storm."

Steven spent another four weeks in the hospital, and they thought it was quite miraculous that he left there alive. By the time he got home, my emotions about the truth were settled. There were going to be some changes around our home. My brother Stevie stayed after Mommie and Bo left. He stayed to help me around the house and to lend a hand when Steven finally came home.

It turned out that while Steven was in the hospital barking out orders to make this purchase and that, he had been in the midst of one of his demented episodes. He would swing back and forth between periods of lucidity and lunacy. When he got home and started going through the mail, he flipped out when he saw the credit card bills. I mean flipped!

He cussed me out for shopping and buying stuff for the house. He got on the phone and called everyone in his

family to report that I was trying to kill him early by bringing all of this financial stress on him. Here's the kicker: he
never even *remembered* telling me that he was going to file
bankruptcy and to go shopping.

"That's a joke!" he fumed. "Why would I do that, so
some other nigger can come up in here when I'm gone and
you all can laugh at me for being a sucker while you enjoy
this stuff you bought? Why would I want to make life easy
for you when I'm gone!"

"You told me to do this!"

"It wasn't a done deal," he said. "You shouldn't have
done it."

I was beginning to see clearly now. All too clearly.
Either Steven was truly going through bouts of dementia
or he had serious game. I chalked it up to both, in light of
my newfound truth.

"I need to get away from you," he said. "I don't have
that much time left and I don't want to be here in this
cold. I want to go out to California with my godmother and
die out there where it's warm."

"Really? And what about your doctor's appointments? And who's going to take care of you?" I asked him,
concerned because Godmother Martha may have been a
nurse, but that didn't mean that she could do what I had
been doing for him with all of my concoctions.

"They'll do a better job than you, 'cause these bills are
causing me nothing but stress," he said, flinging the bills
in my face. "Now where's the fur coat you bought?"

"It's still at the shop," I told him.

"Well, return it!" he screamed.

"I'll be returning every single thing I bought," I said. "See, I didn't want to do this in the first place, but *nooooo*, you wanted me to get this and that. So I tell you what, I'll take it all back, gift certificates included. 'Cause it ain't nothing but stuff to me."

"I told everybody in my family what you did," he said.

"Good, now you can tell them I returned it all," I shouted as I started gathering things to put near the front door, including all of the gift certificates. "Never mind, I'll tell them myself!"

I stomped upstairs, slammed the door, and went to bed.

He must have stayed up all night talking to my brother. He must have stayed up even after Stevie went to sleep, because there was not one gift certificate to be found in the house when I woke up. To this day, I don't know to whom he gave so many gift certificates. There were only a handful of people coming to the house regularly. Claudette and Stacey said that he didn't give the certificates to them, so I still have no idea.

I knew about these types of episodes, and it was my fault for not recognizing the dementia in him sooner. It was very sad seeing him slowly lose his motor skills (he flipped over the truck, totaling it) and also watching him lose his mental capacity. It was killing me deep down.

I wrote the family this following letter of apology:

31 January 1995

Dear Family:
It's ironic I write a letter on this day. Steven and I met this very day in 1990. By now I'm sure you all know what I have done recently that has caused Steven a great deal of stress. I am writing to say to all of you that I never in a million years intended to hurt him and to say that I'm sorry.

My rationale for doing these things is not elementary at all. It goes beyond my being selfish, which is just the emotion/action that is on the surface. But what is really underneath it is a severe panic, fear, loneliness. You all are not intimate as I am with what is going on with him and the disease. I'm now well read on the subject and I should have noticed this end-stage dementia before I went shopping.

I've seen you all recently and you've commented on my strength during this ordeal. I guess I've got you all fooled because that is the biggest facade imaginable. That strength characteristic is a face I put on every day to make it. I put on strength so I don't break down and cry, kick, scream and holler in front of Steven and have him to worry even more. So I do my crying each time I leave this house in the car. I break down in public places. I excuse myself from my desk daily to run to the bathroom or I sit there staring out of the window, tears streaming, hoping no one sees me "doing that again."

So what do I do? I tell all of you and even others that I'm doing okay and not to worry. When that is a lie above all lies. But what do I really say? Do I share the litany that I live daily? Can I really scream out loud to say how much this is

*killing me? So I say all is well. Not just to you all but to ev-
erybody. So when it finally came down to me cracking up, I
didn't jump up and down, I didn't warn anybody, I didn't run
off for days unable to be found, I didn't go jump in the sack
with some stranger to ease my pain. I went shopping after I
was told to go by Steven.*

*Steven says that I had to have put a lot of thought into
where I went to make those kinds of purchases. But I will tell
you that is not true. I simply got in the car and started driving
and charged wherever I landed. For a period of a week and a
half I know I went completely crazy. I thought Steven would
be pleased by having the basement fixed so I took care of that
first. Because even though the doctors were saying he wasn't
coming home after five seizures and a collapsed lung, I knew
he was.*

*Even though he had discussed bankruptcy, nothing was
final yet. I rationalized the buying like everything was ap-
proved and a done deal. He says I didn't cover my tracks very
well. That's because I wasn't trying to sneak. I'm not a good
liar. Never have been. I've never been sneaky. My eyes reveal
too much.*

*So from that time, to the time Steven got the bills in the
mail, I was a nervous wreck. If I would have been in a right
state in the first place I would have never bought one thing to
add to the pressures of what we deal with here daily. It was an
intermittent escape. That's the best way I can describe the
feeling at the time.*

*Escapade completed. Reality still here, and back to my
daily routine as follows: get in car and cry all the way to work*

and home; be scared to come in the house because I don't know if Steven will be in here dead or not; cry because you go to sleep one day and the next your whole life is turned upside down; fight with Social Services about why we can't get food stamps, cash assistance or Medicaid even though we've worked our entire lives; go to doctor's appointments and listen to them tell me Steven doesn't have long; write letters to creditors about Steven's disability to ask for reduction in monthly payments; cry about Steven's immobility, face breakouts, lack of appetite, dementia, shrinking frame; coordinate neighbors to check in so he won't be here alone all day; guard his privacy—keep straight in my head who knows who doesn't know; help him go to the bathroom; making the bed finding blood-stained sheets; call doctor because blood is a problem; don't forget latex gloves wash blood-stained stuff separately, bleach first; cry, that in sickness and in health stuff is for real; pay a few bills—mortgage first; look for a job; go to an interview; grocery shop—don't forget chocolate milk and cinnamon pop tarts, it's the only thing I can count on Steven consuming; wash his hair; check in on him in middle of the night—temperature may get too high, he still insists on sleeping with the heat blaring; cry, because he's always cold; order more wood, pick up more coal, call electric company, make payment arrangements the bill is $800!!!; feed Missy and Rambo; pay neighbor to feed and walk them after school, Steven is too weak; cry, the dogs are his pride but he can't really enjoy them; love him so much wish I could take some of the pain; cry because I know I can't; chase down station wagon car payment from source, convinced it was a bad busi-

ness deal but we can't pay so better late than never; cry because I need to get a better paying job to help rescue us from the system that we can't get into anyhow and to get the best doctors without having to worry about how to pay the bill; go to Brooklyn twice a month to get $200 medicine for free; medical bills can't pay; other bills use them to start the fires in the wood-burning stove; cry, bill collectors calling from 8 a.m. to 10 p.m. getting on my nerves; get a new phone number; cry, there are a lot of people we will never remember to call to give them the new number; have to go on a business trip, I hate to leave Steven alone; call home, machine picks up, mind races cry myself into an almost sleep, race home relieved he's still here; cry, he talks about the strangest things, about wanting his mother, how she will make everything all right and take care of him; concentrate, begin on next book; cry, want to write about these emotions but I don't want anybody to see what I'm feeling; maybe an article about our situation would help some people, can't do it—need to guard his privacy; go to post office, sign for certified letters, getting hauled into court for not paying a contractor; cry, money/bills stress Steven; need to go to church or Bible study, can't, don't want to leave Steven alone—pray at home, watch the preachers on TV and read my Bible; looking forward to nephews Robbie and Cory's visit for the holidays; cry, no kids of our own; get up at 6 a.m. clean wood and coal stoves, dump in more coal, start fire, wash dishes, put in a load of clothes, make lunch for Steven, label and leave in fridge, feed and take out dogs, bathe, get dressed, get in the car and cry.

These are just a few of the emotions that are locked up

under the "I'm doing okay" facade. We've got two choices here and that is to deal or to deny. I'm trying to deal. I broke down for a period and now I'm back and returning the purchases.

God forgives me; I hope you will, too.

Love you all . . . LaJoyce

Steven was flabbergasted that I actually sent a letter to his sisters, uncle, godmother, and cousins.

"Let's see who returns those gift certificates you passed out," I told him. "You wanna tell everyone our business, let's tell it *all*. Why do they only get to hear your story? You do realize I have a story in all of this, too?"

Uncle Charles was the only one who called me to say anything about it.

"I'm praying for you," he said earnestly.

For me, that was all he needed to say and it sealed our relationship forever.

When Stevie left to return to Chicago, he gave me a gun tour in my own house. He said he watched Steven look at a gun in the office one night and then hide it.

"I figured that chump had a gun hidden in every room of this house, and I was right," my brother told me. "You be careful, and let me show you the new places every room has a gun."

Stevie was showing me the hiding places. He was tearful when leaving and let me know that he could be there by car in ten hours anytime, day or night.

"Just call," he said.

Stevie was absolutely on target to move those guns away from Steven. Two days later he said, "I think that little brother of yours was stealing from us while he was here."

"Really, what's missing?" I asked, thinking he discovered something missing for real other than guns.

"I don't know yet, but I bet he took something."

"Let me know what's missing and I'll tell Mommie to take it out of his behind!" I said to him.

Later that night, I took a peek at all of the new hiding places, and all of the guns were still nicely tucked away where my little brother had left them. I just let Steven continue to think that Stevie stole the guns from our home. He didn't mention it again, and neither did I.

In the middle of the Pocono winter, Steven left home one day in the truck and called me later that night to say he was in Long Island and would be staying with his sisters for two weeks because he needed to get away from me.

"Okay, make sure they do everything for you that I do," I said to make sure he would stay well.

"Oh, they will," he assured.

Hmm, I thought. *Suddenly they were all getting along and were going to take care of him?*

When did this happen? Since we began the vicious merry-go-round with hospitals and doctors, I could count how many times they came to visit. Never once bringing a bag of groceries, a prepared meal, or offering respite to me. Instead, they'd bounce in from the Long Island haul—and the three-hour trip was a haul—hungry and ravaging my pots and refrigerator, leaving a dirty kitchen and dishes in their wake.

So I needed to be forgiven if I was wrong about them taking good care of him all of a sudden, when because of their glaring absence, they didn't even know how to care for him in this condition.

"If you wanted to spend time with your sisters, I would have taken you out there. Why did you drive out there by yourself?" I questioned him because it was very obvious he was a candidate to have his license revoked due to health issues.

"Because of what you did," he said. "I couldn't stand looking at you another day."

"Whatever, Steven," I said. "You may not remember telling me to shop, but I have Stevie, Bo Daddy, and little Cory to corroborate my story. And I bet I can find a nurse or two who heard you giving me a shopping list. Don't forget you were thirty thousand dollars in debt when I met you, that *we* have been paying down since we got married. You've barely made a dent in that. The twenty thousand dollars I've just spent is not only returnable, but a joke compared to the debt you already had. They can all vouch for the fact that you appeared to be lucid at the time you told me to go!"

"There you go using big words," he said, irritated. "What's 'lucid'?"

"If you're well enough to drive three hours to Long Island, then you can pick up a dictionary and find out," I told him.

Steven hated to read and never even bothered to read one pamphlet about his illness. I did all of the reading and researching.

I had started to think that he was running a game with me about the degree of his weakness. Here's a shell of a man who claimed he could barely walk, let alone pack the largest suitcase in the house and make a three-hour trip. I seriously wondered.

He had ordered me to come out there that weekend with items he needed to take to California.

"I'll drive the Honda out and switch for the truck when I get there," I advised.

"No, you won't," he said. "I told my sister she could drive the truck while I was gone."

"Whaaat?! And what am I supposed to drive when it snows and I can't get off of the mountain to get to work to *pay* for the truck *she's* driving?" I asked. "What exactly am I supposed to do then?"

"Whatever you have to, but the truck stays here."

I had a huge concert event with George Howard that weekend in the city and in Long Island at Westbury Music Fair. GH was on a smooth jazz tour with Grover Washington Jr., Phil Perry, and Dianne Reeves, and they were killing audiences all around the country. When GH saw me, he knew I was totally stressed because I had lost a considerable amount of weight.

GH took my face in his hands and his eyes welled up.

"You can hide it over the phone, baby sis, but you can't hide it in front of me any longer," he said. "What's up?"

He knew Steven was sick, but he had the stomach cancer story.

"I'll tell you later," I answered, looking around at all of the people backstage.

"Stop playing, you'll tell me now," he said, concerned, and turned me his ear.

I whispered the truth. He covered his face and cried right backstage at Westbury Music Fair. We hugged and I assured him that I was definitely negative and my weight loss was indeed from stress. My photographer for the evening, Ronnie Wright, saw us huddled and told us to smile. I have the most beautiful photo of us with GH's watery eyes.

I spent the night with Steven's sisters at the house they were renting. With all of the money they got between the two of them, instead of pooling it toward owner-ship, they chose to rent. Go figure. One look in their re-frigerator and I knew Steven was not being fed the right way. There was a load of chocolate milk, and bananas. There was no other fruit and no salad fixings, so I knew he hadn't eaten any. I had brought groceries, the things he needed to eat and bags of herbs I had premixed so that they just had to add hot water.

Steven was pulling a not-speaking-to-me episode that weekend. It took so much more effort to be nasty than it did to be nice.

Before leaving on Sunday, I gave him an egg facial be-cause his face was all broken out. I told him while he had his mask on and couldn't talk back, "I'm glad to see that you and your sisters are speaking. Please patch up all the way and discuss everything you want to talk about that has had you angry. And I hope you're not here just because you're angry with me."

He may have been mad with me, but he didn't pass up the pampering session. I told him I had brought enough herbs to take to California and supplements as well. I labeled everything and sent an instruction sheet.

The sisters just said, "We'll try. We don't have time to do all of this."

"I love you and have fun when you go to California," I said before leaving. "See you when you get back."

"I told you I was going out there to die. I'm not coming back," he said adamantly.

I got a flash of the wedding video again as I left those siblings to themselves: "He's your problem now; don't send him back to our house!"

There was an eerie peace that enveloped my home in the Poconos after Steven left. He had refused to speak to me on the phone and I didn't know what his exact travel plans were. I got a lot of rest and started looking for another job. I hated to leave Patti's fold, but I needed more money or we were going to lose everything. Having a dying husband was expensive! I was only writing five checks a month and it was tight.

I was on payment arrangements with everyone, and if the payment was not on time with the phone company, they would shut off the long distance service. I was diligent, but it happened anyway.

Patti didn't have enough money to pay us one Friday because a client didn't pay. I had already mailed the bills before coming to work that morning. Three days later, I only had incoming service. It was GH who came to my rescue. He allowed me to use his telephone calling card to make calls until I got myself straightened out.

Godmother Martha called me to let me know Steven had been there three days and that he was really weak, but she would take care of him. I knew that was gospel. While he was gone, I got myself back on track with church and Bible study, and it felt good to be among my church family, who had been praying for me.

In April 1995, my longtime industry friend Jackie called me up to let me know of an opening at Arista Records as publicity manager in New York City. I jumped at the chance. I didn't even know how much the salary was, but it didn't matter. I needed a job with benefits, because I didn't have any.

In my interview process, I had to tell them about my dying husband at home with stomach cancer. They needed to know he was in the final stages and that when the time came for me to be near him, I would have to be absent.

"No problem at all," my vice president said, visibly wrecked by the news.

She even kissed me good-bye. She was also very impressed with the fact that I took the interview just off of the plane, with luggage in tow, returning from a benefit GH held in Atlanta for the Clark Atlanta University band.

"I knew I liked you, a woman who's not afraid to travel," she marveled.

When she told me the salary would be thirty-five

thousand dollars, I almost fell out of my chair, because the week before at Bible study, Pastor K.P. had delivered an awesome prophecy.

He interrupted his teaching by saying, "If anyone can give thirty-five dollars right now, come up here and place it on the altar. I'm going to anoint your purse, your wallet . . . and in the next seven days, God is saying that he will increase you tenfold, some of you one-hundred-fold, some of you one-thousand-fold."

I usually take issue with pastors who say give this to get that, but Pastor K.P. would dismiss church and forget to raise the offering and we'd all have to put our envelopes in a basket upon leaving. So I knew it wasn't about "raising" money. What was interesting is that before coming to church I went to the store for fruit and veggies with only a fifty-dollar bill. I asked the cashier for all fives back from my less-than-ten-dollar purchase, and I didn't know why. I took the I-don't-know-why feeling as a direct communication from God.

When Pastor K.P. made that call, I was among the first up to the altar. He told me, "Go get your purse." I brought up my backpack and he asked, "Is this where you keep your money?"

"Yes," I answered, and the congregation laughed.

He ordered, "Don't laugh at her! If this is where she keeps her money, then this bag gets anointed!" My leather backpack got all greased up with blessed oil and I went praising all the way home. Approximately six days later, the thirty-five dollars was increased one-thousand-fold. I just wished I had bought that tape of the sermon!

After we sealed the Arista start date, I bounced onto West Fifty-seventh Street and praised the Lord.

My new job was absolutely awesome! I was publicity manager and my roster included Craig Mack, Biggie Smalls (a.k.a. The Notorious B.I.G.), his wife Faith Evans, Sean "Puffy" Combs (as he was known back then), Total, 112, OutKast, and Toni Braxton.

It was fast-paced to the nth power! I had an assistant named Samantha and she marveled at how I juggled three phone lines simultaneously. When you receive two hundred and fifty calls a day, there is no way you can call anybody back. If someone calls you, put them on hold and get to them quickly.

My first task at Arista was to plan a rap party that was to happen in one week, for a deejay compilation CD. The only thing done for the event was identifying its location. I loved this work and I definitely needed the diversion.

I was summoned home to Chicago one weekend for a much-needed visit alone with my folks. All I did was sit in my room and stare out of my window, thinking. My mother would come up to the room with a different beverage— juice, iced tea, or a peach wine cooler. What she brought to drink would determine what kind of conversation we'd have.

Steven still wasn't speaking to me. Every time I called California, he would say he was tired and then get off of the phone. Godmother Martha told me that I might want to consider coming out there to visit him, because she knew it was near the end.

My mother and I did a lot of talking and thanking God about what He had done in my life. I know she just wanted to see her baby for a minute in her house. "Grounding" is what you call it—returning to the point of safety. My grounding point was my room at Mommie's house.

Before I left for church on Sunday, the Holy Spirit told me to get to Gus's house to pray for Daddy Brookshire, who had recently gone blind. I went there to lay hands on Daddy's eyes and pray for his healing.

"I have a surprise for you," Mama Brookshire said, dialing the phone. "Gus Brookshire's room, please."

"Are Gus and his wife in town?" I wanted to know.

Mama Brookshire hesitated and fumbled for words. "No . . . well, he . . ."

I've known the Brookshires most of my life from the neighborhood, and Mama Brookshire has never been one short of words. I knew something was wrong.

"My boy ain't washing no hair!" Daddy Brookshire piped up angrily.

"Washing hair?" I asked. "What is going on?"

Gus and his wife owned a salon in San Antonio, and the last time we spoke, they had just bought a fabulous new home. The last I had heard, their place was the number-two black salon in town. Gus had quit his job as a land surveyor to manage both the construction of the new deluxe space and the day-to-day operations. It was very plain to see that Daddy Brookshire was perturbed at the prospect of *any*one wanting his boy to wash hair, considering all Gus had sacrificed.

I mused to myself, *Mmmmm, seems someone feels Gus needs to do more than just manage the place.*

Mama handed me a piece of paper. "Call your brother at this number when you get home tonight. It will be nice for him to speak to his sister."

As promised, I called Gus when I got back to the Poconos.

"What did Mama and Daddy tell you?" he asked.

"Daddy said something about you 'not washing no hair,' and Mama just asked me to call you."

"I'm getting a divorce," he said, exhaling.

He told me the longest story, and all I could say when he was finished was "Wow!"

Gus was a real doer of the Word of God. He was totally against divorce, but his wife committed adultery with one of their employees' relatives at the salon. He had moved out and enrolled in a truck-driving school in Dallas. I sat in shocked silence as I listened to his story for more than an hour. For a change, it felt good to be of support to another in a difficult situation, rather than being wrapped up in my own.

"What about you?" he asked.

I didn't really want to discuss it, but Gus was my first-ever best friend, so I told him the truth about Steven.

"I know everything already," he said, blowing me away. "Stevie called me at home in the middle of the night to ask me to come there to help kill your husband for what he was doing to you." In my family's eyes, Steven's disease was ruining my life.

See, my family is crazy, I thought.

Gus continued, "I spent two hours talking your brother down from killing him that night by telling him I'd come if he would wait for me to get there. I knew that he'd simmer down."

I started to cry, because the impact of this ordeal on me, my family, and my friends was just too much. I wasn't prepared to deal with any of it anyway, and now I had to help my family deal with something I wasn't sure how to navigate myself. It was only by the grace of God that I was functioning at all. Steven's diagnosis had driven my brother to call Gus and ask for his help in *killing him*. That's no small thing! I couldn't believe it. That's why my brother stayed around; he stayed to protect me. Between the Blood of Jesus *and* Stevie, all bases were covered.

We talked for three hours, crying and praying, and reading Bible scriptures to each other for comfort. Gus had been nearby for every major event in my life, and while we had not spoken in a long time, I felt his genuine support and familiar comfort envelop me.

That Friday, I had a cold and was turning out the lights to go to bed when Missy started barking at the door. Steven had arrived in the truck with his sister.

"Look who's home, Missy," I said, holding her collar to let them inside.

I welcomed them both, helped to get Steven settled, and offered food. Steven was dangerously thin, his face was a broken-out mess, and he was walking shakily. The two of them barely looked my way or even said anything to me.

"I have a bad cold, so I was about to go to bed," I said.

"Steven, you can sleep in our bedroom and I'll sleep in the guest room so you won't catch my germs."

"Where's my sister going to sleep if you sleep in the guest room?" he asked.

"Have you forgotten that there are two other rooms— an office with a futon and a pull-out couch in the TV room?" I said. "She can sleep wherever she wants."

I knew what the deal was. He had decided to sneak up on me unannounced to see if I was going to be home with someone else or even home at all. Missy and I went to the guest room, and I heard Steven and his sister watching TV most of the night.

Saturday morning arrived with my usual flurry of activities, and I was out of the house by seven. Steven was always a late riser. I could go to town, run several errands, get back home, and cook breakfast all before he ever woke up.

I left Steven at home and went to work. I'd left food labeled in the fridge and medicines lined up on the counter. When I got home that night the house was completely dark.

I sat in the car a moment and prayed, "Lord, please don't let him be in this house dead. I have three requests: One, please don't let me come home and find him dead. Two, please don't let him die in this house. And three, don't let me be there when he dies. Amen."

These were not unreasonable requests; there are some things I'd rather not remember. I would hate to have to think, *This is the room I found him in*, or watch him take his last breath. Some people are okay with being there in the last moments. I felt that was a job for a professional. I was already wiped out emotionally. I didn't need anything else to rattle me. I was sure God would honor the requests I had made in earnest, and I went into the house.

Steven had slept all day without eating or drinking anything. He said he was very tired and cold. In spite of its traditionally warm weather, California was in the midst of a rainy cold snap that lasted for the duration of his two-month visit. Day in and day out he complained that he was freezing. I gave him an herbal concoction laced with cayenne pepper to get his blood circulating. When I checked his extremities, sure enough, they were blue.

I took him to the emergency room, and he stayed in the hospital three days. The doctor just shook his head, because he could not believe Steven was still alive.

"All indicators of his tests show that he should not still be here," he said. "On paper, he's technically dead already. It's just a matter of time. He has an ironclad will. I've seen how he treats you, and it seems as if he's hanging on just so he can punish you for some reason."

That was an incredible revelation from a doctor—an outsider who saw us only once a month.

He's punishing me for being negative, I thought.

I wrecked Steven's plan by not contracting AIDS and riding into the sunset to die with him. So he was trying his best to make me miserable while he waited to die.

CHAPTER SEVEN

The Preparation for Death

When calamity comes, the wicked are brought down,
but even in death the righteous have a refuge.

—PROVERBS 14:32

When Steven came home from the hospital, I made arrangements to leave food in a cooler in the bedroom so he could easily get to his provisions. I was trying to do everything I could to make sure he was comfortable and did not have to get up from bed.

One day my assistant rushed me out of a meeting to tell me Steven was on the phone with an emergency.

"Rabbit, I need you to come home," he said, crying.

I braced myself. "What happened?"

"I went to the bathroom, and when I got off of the toilet I fell down," he said. "I couldn't get up off the floor, so I had to drag myself to the bed, and it took almost an hour to do it because I'm so weak. I need you to come home now! I need you!"

"I'm on the way," I said.

I opened the door to my vice president's office and simply stated, "Emergency," and she nodded.

On the bus home, I put into action what I knew now needed to be done. I was working, and Steven was clearly in no shape to be home alone all day. I thought of Ruthie. She and Clive had split up, and she was staying with a friend. She immediately said yes to my offer for her to move in.

When I relayed the details of Steven's episode to the doctor, he told me the neuropathy (a loss of sensation in the extremities) was no longer just a threat but in full effect. That was the last day Steven walked.

A neighbor came in the next day every two hours to check on Steven until I could get home with the full-time help. Ruthie got settled into the guest room and was happy to be away from the city and her situation for a while. Her breakup had been happening right under my nose, and I'd never even noticed the decline in their relationship. She and God let me know it was a good thing that I was so intensely taking care of my own house that I didn't notice what was happening anywhere else.

Steven loved Ruthie very much, but he was displeased with the new arrangement. He reamed me up and down for not taking a leave of absence to care for him myself.

"And who is going to pay the mortgage and the electric heating bill if I take a leave?" I asked.

"You know you can ask your parents," he said. "They'll help you."

"Sure they will, but I'm not asking," I said. "My parents are retired, and they are enjoying themselves on the

beaches of the world because they deserve it. I'm not load-
ing anything extra on them. This is *my* cross to bear. The
money can be easily made, but I've got to go to work."

He made no bones about his displeasure with this
arrangement. It was a good thing that I loved working at
Arista so much, because there was no way I could be in
the house with Steven twenty-four/seven. Since the day he
came home from California, I had been sleeping in the
guest room. He was so needy throughout the night that I'd
spend most of it running up and down the hall to comply
with his requests. Finally, I made a soft pallet on the floor
at the foot of his bed.

Steven literally woke me up every hour so that I could
be of service to him.

"I've got to use the bathroom," he'd say, which usually
meant using a urinal. He had been using a urinal for a long
time, and since urine is a body fluid and the virus is transmitted through body fluids, it had to be handled like blood.

Miss Lucille had sent me a basket with assorted
essentials to conduct at-home care. There were all sorts of
creams, sprays, and ointments to prevent Steven's skin
from becoming dry and developing bedsores. The most
important items were the latex gloves. Just like the hospital employees, I wore the gloves when I took care of him.

"I'm thirsty," he'd whine, waking me in the middle of
the night.

I still maintained his well-stocked cooler next to the
bed. He didn't need to ask me for anything cold to drink
during the night. He could reach it himself.

"I want cinnamon toast," he would say an hour later.

Steven consumed large quantities of cinnamon toast day and night, alternately with cinnamon-frosted Pop-Tarts, because I refused to let him eat that junk food ten times a day.

I knew that the virus loved and thrived on sugar, which is why he kept having thrush in his mouth. Thrush is a condition that arises due to an overrun of yeast (candida) in the body. The yeast then settles in a moist, dark place and festers, and at times it can manifest itself in the mouth. If not properly controlled, too much candida could cause a systemic yeast problem, which compounds any initial diagnosis. Ultimately, the culprits of such a yeast infection are the nasty whites—pasta, rice, white sugar, and flour.

Steven had a lifetime love affair with sweets. Claudette remembers that he had a bag of assorted candy the first day she met him, in the 1980s. I did my best to educate him on the importance of nutrition in addition to medication. He would *not* listen. He also knew that he could manipulate Ruthie into giving him whatever he wanted to eat.

He would tell me, "I'm dying! Why do you care what I eat?! Why can't you just let me have some happiness? These are my last days, and you're depriving me of the food I love. I hate you!"

I'd heard the "I hate you" line spewed at me before, as well as at his sisters or about them. Steven was so angry at so many people; it was a shame to see my husband this bitter. His already-sour disposition festered into a toxic-waste pool that he no longer concealed.

"You think just because Ruthie is here to help me that

I'm letting you off the hook in taking care of me?" he would say as he woke me up every hour during the night. "There is no way you're getting a break. I'm going to make you do your wifely duties."

"Don't ever think you're making me do *any*thing," I would remind him calmly. "Now, what can I get you?"

The ninety-minute bus rides to and from New York City were the only uninterrupted sleep I would get every day. Taking care of Steven was like having a newborn baby, but I had heard that infants at least woke up every *two* hours. I was bordering on exhaustion, and a couple of times I'd slept past my stop at the Port Authority on Forty-second Street and rode to the end of the line at the World Trade Center. I would have to take the subway back to midtown, but I never minded, because the sleep I'd gotten on the bus had been so good.

At work one day, the president of black music, Jean Riggins, asked to speak with me. I grabbed a pad and ran down the hall to her office. There sat the two vice presidents of black music—Lionel and David—and Jean's assistant, Michelle.

"Sit down," Jean ordered. The formality of it all had me thinking I was about to be fired. My heart was pounding.

Jean leaned over her desk and looked me square in the eye.

"Why is it that we are just finding out you have a terminally ill husband at home who is very close to death?" she asked.

I exhaled. *Oh, that,* I said to myself, knowing they had the stomach cancer story.

"I'm sorry," I said. "I thought you all knew."

"No, we all just found out this morning," Jean said. "How come you didn't say anything?"

Lionel, who had been looking out the window, turned to me. "No, what I want to know is, how is it that you are the brightest spot up in here and you're going through all this? I depend on seeing your smile every day!" he said, pointing at me, complimenting my disposition while at the same time perplexed about my trouble.

David interjected, "You keep us all smiling and upbeat no matter what, and you've got this to deal with?"

Michelle stood at the edge of the desk with her hand over her mouth in shock, rocking back and forth.

"You guys, this is no place for me to wear what's happening at home on my face," I said. "I've got a job to do—"

"Which you do well," Lionel interrupted.

"Thank you," I said. "I have to leave my house every day to have some sanity. I have full-time help, and I don't start thinking about home again until I get off the bus and drive the twenty-two miles to my house. I basically start thinking about whether or not I will come inside and find him dead."

Michelle whispered, "Oh, my God!"

"I cannot carry a thought like that around with me all day. I thank you all for your concern, but I'm God's Girl, for real. He's got me."

"Well, you're our girl, too," Jean said. "And it's killing

us to hear you going through all of this. I don't know what to do to help. I'm going to give you a check for two hundred dollars. Can that help you?"

I started to get misty.

"Yes, it will. Thank you so much," I said, thinking of putting a dent into the phone bill to get the outgoing service restored.

"Good," she said, writing a check. "And if you need some more, you better let me know."

I hugged them, excused myself, and went to my desk to cry until I was interrupted by Ruthie calling. She was crying. Fortunately, Arista had an 800 number, so that call could be made from home without using George's calling card.

For Ruthie to call me at work crying while she was at home caring for my dying husband was not a good sign.

"What happened?" I asked.

"Girrrrrl," she sniffled. "Steven has gone crazy."

"Yes, of course, he has dementia on top of a raging case of entitlement," I said. "That's a lethal combination."

"Joycie, as much as I'd like to stay, I can't," she said. "At first, I wasn't going to tell you. It's been going on for a week now, but he cussed me out until I cried today, telling me how fat I was and that he couldn't stand the sight of me. And he told me to leave him alone, that you would do what needed to be done for him when you got home. And he sees now why Clive and I broke up. And how I would never find anyone to love me again the way he did because no one wants a fat wife."

"I'm so sorry, honey," I said, trying to comfort her.

Steven said all of these things to her because he knew they would hit a nerve. Ruthie weighed about three hundred pounds, and I loved every ounce of her. She had a heart of gold that matched her lively personality.

I saw straight through Steven. He was trying to sabotage my efforts to provide care for him until I exhausted all of the possibilities and had to do it myself.

"I rebuke you in the name of Jesus," I said out loud.

Looking over at me, my assistant knew there was trouble. By now she was used to hearing me praising Jesus right at my desk.

Ruthie said, "I'm going to call Kim to pick me up tonight, so you don't have to take me to the city."

Even in her departure, and as bad as Steven had treated her, she thought of me first by making arrangements to be picked up from the Poconos.

I got right on the phone, made a master calendar, and put Plan B into action. First thing: get coverage for the next day. Pastor K.P. volunteered, making himself available every Wednesday.

Great—Wednesday's done, I thought.

Pastor K.P. had done us a huge favor by using one of our cars and taking over the payments. We had two cars and two trucks, and it was very hard to juggle all of the finances. Pastor K.P. loved the Taurus station wagon and cared for it like it was his own.

By the time I got home that night, I had a calendar of caregivers, day by day. Then I told Steven off for hurting the feelings of my dear friend.

I went over the new calendar with Steven and showed

him I had booked caregivers two months out. Tyger would give up her vacation for a week, along with cousin Mayla. Henzy from Indianapolis would come for ten days. My godsister Sloopy and dance-buddy/cousin Pam would come for a few days, and of course, the parents would come for a week. Stacey and Claudette were already coming every weekend, primarily for Stacey to put Steven into the sunken tub for a long soak.

None of Steven's family and friends other than Stacey were available for this intensive duty of at-home care. Some weekends his sisters did what I called drive-by visits, coming to the Poconos from Long Island and returning the same day. I did understand their plight. Both sisters had two jobs, and the younger was also caring for a toddler—so she had *three* jobs. But I don't care what went down in their lifetimes, in the last couple of years, or even yesterday—their brother was dying a slow and painful death. It was a hard reality to view, but the least they could have done was be more present.

Steven protested, "I don't know what it's gonna take for you to get a leave of absence and come home to take care of me."

"Forget it," I said.

Work, with all of its insanity, was a blip on the radar compared to Steven. I wasn't trying to leave the work of caring for him to others while I did nothing, but my friends who knew the situation helped out in order to rescue me. God had already saved me more than once, and my family and friends were saving me from the rest.

They all got an orientation about how to care for Steven and for themselves.

Mayla and Tyger were an awesome combo. Taking care of a bed-bound grown man took a strong stomach and physical strength. Mayla had to excuse herself when I showed them how to position Steven for bowel movements. He refused to wear diapers anymore, saying he didn't want the feces on himself. So Steven would lie on his right side and release the excrement onto a disposable bed lining. He then had to be wiped, cream had to be applied and sealed with the spray, and the waste had to be carefully rolled up and disposed. Tyger would show up in the room with gloves and a mask, because you never knew what the request would be when you were called. That was a good idea, and everyone started following suit.

Mayla and Tyger made Steven eat, be nice, and talk about all the things he was feeling but didn't think he could tell me.

After about three days, Mayla and Tyger had an intervention with me when I got home in the evening. First they were very complimentary about the job I was doing. In spite of his condition, Steven was well cared for and holding on.

"From now on, you must have at least two people here at all times," Tyger said emphatically.

Mayla agreed. "This is too much for any one person to handle. The cooking, running up and down the stairs, being careful all the time. I don't know how you do it, LaJoyce."

"By the grace of God," I told them.

Tyger maintained her emphatic posture. "Either have two people here always, or it's time to get a nurse."

The next day I looked into getting a nurse through the insurance company. Sure enough, Steven was eligible for one. I was thankful for Tyger's suggestion. My brain was so fried that sometimes I wasn't as on-the-ball as I needed to be. Since I wasn't getting enough sleep, I tripled my health regimen and made sure that I stayed away from any sugar, which could weaken my immune system.

I was sad to see Tyger go, but she was a sweetie for giving up her vacation. Since she was a flight attendant, I knew the last thing she wanted to do was get on a plane so she could serve someone hand and foot when that is what she did all day long.

"I'll be waiting for the day when you call me and all I hear on the other end is you crying," she said, grabbing my face in her hands. "You won't have to say anything, you won't have to apologize. I'll know it's you, and that day is coming."

We cried our eyes out.

Mayla came every weekend after her one-week visit. I was worried about her doing all of that late-night running up and down I-80 from New York to be with me, but she confessed, "I love you very much, and I can't watch you going through all of this by yourself."

Even though Mayla and I are cousins, we are more like sisters. She is actually my second cousin and my father Duke's first cousin. But she and I are closer in age, and our similar spiritual walk makes us even closer.

It was great having so many people come to help out, but my kitchen arrangement was in a shambles. I couldn't find anything. During a long, boring conference call at work, I made labels for the cabinets to help keep everyone organized. That put an end to getting calls at work from caregivers asking where we kept things like the hot sauce.

The registered nurse, Tracey, came first thing every morning to check Steven's vitals. Tracey lived in our community, just a little more than a mile from our house. God sure worked that one out. The nurse's aides were scheduled for five hours a day.

Better than nothing, I thought. This meant that friends who were helping us would not have to run around for five hours.

Henzy arrived to find Steven unable to keep anything down. He was throwing up constantly, and the doctor feared that the sarcoma was spreading to his intestinal lining. The breakouts on Steven's face were a result of Kaposi's sarcoma, a type of skin cancer that is a by-product of AIDS for some people. The sarcoma was ever present, and I continued to conduct the skin care regimen because Steven loved it. The truth was that he had begun to look like he had leprosy—not that any of us had ever seen a leper, but the Bible is descriptive enough to give our imaginations license to run wild.

Steven was scheduled for an immediate procedure in which a probe with a camera was inserted down his throat and his intestines were viewed on a screen. The doctor had stressed that if he found lesions, as he suspected he would, Steven would probably die within a few days. I cried my eyes out at the hospital when the doctor made his announcement to us because I was worried about Steven's soul. He had not made any apologies to me for concealing the truth about his illness.

The only person I told about Steven's secret was Henzy. Henzy has the compassion of Jesus on all matters. I knew I could trust him to enter into prayer mode instead of running to find the nearest gun. He was and still is wired very differently from the typical man. Henzy truly exemplifies the love of Jesus every day in every way.

Just as Steven was being rolled into the operating room, Henzy stopped the attendants and prayed with Steven.

"Is there anything you'd like to confess to the Lord right now?" he asked, hoping for truth. "You know that there is nothing you can't tell God. If there is anything at all you'd like to make right with God or with anybody else, now is the time to make that confession."

Steven's eyes bucked wide open. "There is nothing that I can think of I need to confess!"

"Nothing?" Henzy repeated, trying to phrase his question another way. "Then is there anything you need to ask forgiveness of from your wife?"

"Other than I hope she is forgiven for not staying at home to take care of me, there's nothing," Steven said.

Henzy was troubled because it was clear Steven was lying.

"Okay, then. May God be with you," Henzy conceded.

When Steven was rolled away, Henzy took my hand.

"You do know he's never gonna make that confession,

because he's so stubborn," he said. "You're going to have to tell other people about this; we can't let him die without confessing."

The doctor found no lesions in Steven's intestines, but he advised there was nothing more that could be done for him except to keep him comfortable.

"I can recommend a hospice for him in Allentown," he said, giving me the number. "I understand from Steven that you all have made arrangements for him to die at home."

I didn't say anything, but my eyebrow went up and the doctor knew that was a lie. He shook my hand, saying, "Good luck."

Steven complained endlessly about the nurse's aide, saying that she made too much noise in the room while he was trying to sleep and that she was too rough. The agency was kind enough to assign another nurse. I allowed the nurse to remain in other parts of the house, instructing her to enter Steven's room only when summoned or as needed. I wanted to put an end to his complaining about his rest being interrupted.

But there was no longer anything that could control his fevers, shakes, vomiting, thrush, weak muscles, weight loss, or foul disposition. AIDS was ravaging his body with a vengeance.

"Why do you keep taking him to death's door and saving him?" I asked God. "Why are you allowing him to suffer so?"

God said plainly to me, "I've got this, don't ask me again."

It seemed as if I was witnessing one person's hell right here on earth.

Wow, vengeance really is the Lord's, I thought.

My parents rolled in next by car. They proved to be an excellent tag team. By now, everyone knew the truth, and Mommie was furious. It was Henzy's strategy to tell the others to increase the opportunity for Steven's confession. Maybe someone would be able to reach him. The opposite actually happened. It seems as if Steven knew we all knew the truth because we constantly discussed the need to be free from anything that would keep him from entering the gates of Heaven. He became even more cantankerous.

Steven went so far as to tell me, "I don't know what it is, but I no longer trust you."

The magnitude of what he said kicked me in the face. He had a way of doing that. Saying things that were so hurtful it made you sit down. I had a seat on the side of the nightstand and thought very carefully before I said anything.

My mind raced. *Don't trust me!* I screamed in my head. *I'm here still taking care of you and you don't trust me! Let's go back to the first hour we met and you lied to me about some bleeding ulcers. This whole marriage is based on deception! I'm still here, and you want to say you don't trust me.*

Swirling the medicine in the cup I had brought to the room, I contemplated giving him one too many of each or not giving it to him at all. The medications were not helping him to get better, because he was at death's door, but if given too much or none at all, he'd probably die sooner. I thought about how he had come, from a place of deep love, to hate me, and how I had come from deep love to contemplating a decision to take his life.

It was very clear to me—his actions all pointed to the fact that he considered me a nonentity, a vessel to be of service to him in the last days. A body to be a whipping post for him. He wasn't physically able to strike out, but he did it every day with the one strong thing he had left—his tongue. And it had brought me to a place where his fate was absolutely in my hands.

"Yeah, you can't say anything to that," he said, picking at me for not responding to his statement of trust.

He rambled on in the background, but it faded to black as my thoughts of what to do with the medication bounced back and forth in my head like a fierce tennis match between Venus and Serena. I went back to what I know is unchangeable and unmovable, and that is the Word of God.

Whenever I get so angry that I see red, I seek His face right there.

> . . . Well done, thou good and faithful servant; thou has been faithful over a few things, I will make thee ruler over many things; enter thou into the joy of the Lord.
>
> —Matthew 25:21

"Thank you, Jesus," I said aloud, and peace enveloped me.

"Yeah," Steven said dryly. "He's the only one who can help you."

"He's the only one who can help you too, sweetie," I said. "I'm sorry you don't trust me anymore."

"Well, I don't!"

"Well, if I were you, I'd keep that feeling to myself," I said. "How are you going to say something like that to someone who brings you meals and your medicine? It really hurts me to know you don't trust me. Take this"—I handed him the medicine cup—"and *re-think* what you're saying to me."

As he tentatively reached for the cup, I could tell he was thinking about my words. He knew what I was saying, but he didn't say he was sorry. His mistrust of me had settled deep in the bowels of his soul, and he had chosen to let it fester.

I knew that when Steven died, I'd still have to partici-pate in the game of life. How I chose to play it would de-pend largely on how I handled the task before me. If I took the high road, I knew there was a promise at the end of the rainbow made to me by God. If I took the low road, I was setting myself up for a miserable life. The words of Bishop Eddie Long boomed in my memory: "If you don't exhibit faith, you will forever be seated in the misery."

My mother came to Steven's bedroom only to say good morning and good night. Instead of being phony, she chose kitchen duty, churning out meals and keeping the dishes washed, which was a full-time responsibility, for sure. Bo Daddy kept Steven company, doing a lot of talking with him and reading the *Daily Word*, hoping for some glimmer of remorse.

One day I got pulled out of a meeting at work for an emergency call from Mommie about Steven.

"That boy done lost his mind!" she said. "The nurse just came down here in tears saying that in all her fifteen years' experience, she has never been treated like Steven treated her. And she has never been talked to the way he talked to her."

My mother was out of breath and rushing her words together—a sign that she was maaad!

She continued, "That nurse left here crying just now and said she was not coming back!"

I looked at the clock; the nurse was only two hours into her shift.

"What are you going to do?" Mommie asked, but it was more like a demand.

I exhaled. "I'm going to have to call hospice and see if there's a bed available."

"Good, that's what you better do, because he needs professional help," she said. "We've all tried to pitch in, but he's just ridiculous. I don't care if he is sick. He just wants you to do it all. Call hospice now!"

"I will, I will . . . ," I answered reluctantly, because I knew how Steven felt about the whole idea.

"I mean now!" she said. I could just see those huge green eyes of hers threatening me just before flipping into Mommie the green-eyed monster who would snatch you through the phone.

"Right now," I conceded, because my mother's wrath was worse than Steven's. As it turned out, the hospice just happened to have a room available that morning. The ambulance needed to transport him just happened to have a cancellation. And a photo shoot with the fan magazine *Right On!* that I had to do with Usher just happened to be rescheduled. Photo shoots take all day, so there was nothing else on my calendar, making it easy to take off. God wiped out every excuse. He showed me that hospice was the right choice.

I didn't say a word to Steven about where he was going until the ambulance came. Crying like a baby, he asked the ambulance attendants to pause in various parts of the house so that he could get one last look around.

"You do know I'm not coming back," he said to us all. "My wife here is sending me off to die in some strange place."

My mother spoke up. "Haven't we all been here to help you?"

"Yes, I have to admit that you've been here every step of the way. You've made good meals, and Bo's been keeping the jokes coming," he said.

"All right then," Mommie said. "It's just too much for LaJoyce to handle by herself. It's best that you get professional care now, okay?"

Steven asked that I get his pillow, his backrest, and some photos of his mom from the wedding to put in his room. He lingered in the foyer, asking for this and that, stalling. He wanted to pet the dogs right before leaving.

"I'm ready to leave now," he said to the attendants. "Bye-bye, house. I'll never see you again."

Bo and I trailed the ambulance an hour to Allentown. The hospice was beautiful. It almost looked too inviting, luxurious, warm, and comfortable for both family and patient. If ever there was a way to die in a dignified manner, this was it.

Steven loved grandeur, and he was impressed with the place from the lobby to the elevator to his room. He was in rare form, cracking jokes, being the lovable Steven I fell head-over-heels with four years earlier. Bo kept nudging me because Steven was being so nice to everyone and it was a definite shift in his disposition.

"Rabbit, at least you did something right by picking a beautiful place where I'm going to die," Steven complimented me.

We got his room all set up with photos and then stayed the rest of the day. The doctors examined him and commented that if he lasted another seven days it would be a miracle. He was well under one hundred pounds, the sarcoma was all over his face and body, and he was consistently at a temperature of 102.4.

When we were leaving for the evening, I sat on the edge of the bed, pulled him upright, and hugged him close. He told me off for bringing him to his final resting place, but he knew it was for the best.

I phoned the family to let them know Steven was at hospice and probably had only seven days left. I suggested they make their way out to Allentown.

His little sister challenged my decision.

"You know he wants to die at home," she said, lashing out at me.

"You know he's here acting a fool, sending fifteen-year veteran nurses screeching down the mountain, vowing never to return," I said. "He can't die here if there's no help. The at-home program worked until he ran off all of the professional help. Here are the directions to the hospice."

Those girls who showed up every once in a while were *not* going to worry me.

Back at home, Bo Daddy stripped the comforters, bedsheets, and plastic mattress cover, and washed down the mattress with bleach, turned on the ceiling fan, and opened the windows wide. Then he mopped the carpet with a bleach-and-water solution while I lit scented candles.

"I want to see you off of this floor and sleeping in your own bed tonight," Bo Daddy demanded. "Do you hear me?" He scolded me as he continued to disinfect.

The room never did have the feel or smell of a sickroom, but you knew it was one. When Bo Daddy got finished, the room was light and airy. The heaviness was gone. I too felt lighter because I knew Steven was getting care that I couldn't possibly give him.

My parents left a day early, and I made preparations to receive my girls Pam and Sloopy from Chicago for a four-day stay. We were more like family than friends, which is why they were up for duty next. Since my schedule was airtight, no days were uncovered. Even though Steven was in hospice, they still wanted to come. They'd take care of *me*, they said.

I scooped them off of the plane in Allentown, and we went to visit Steven. Busting into the room with her cheery manner, Sloopy brought him a barrel of laughs.

Pam, however, excused herself after five minutes. When she didn't come back in half an hour, I found her in the visitors' lounge crying her eyes out. Her father had recently died of cancer, and I hadn't been able to be there for her.

"I thought I had more time with him," she cried. "I can't do this. I thought I was stronger, but it's bringing up too much emotion."

I hadn't had a chance to properly grieve her father either, and we cried together.

"You know how I loved him," I said. "He taught me how to mix and blend medicinal teas."

Pam's father had lived an organic, holistic lifestyle I had also come to embrace. He always had some tea—one that usually tasted really bad but was really good for you—on their stove and in the fridge. He was so happy when I went to work at GNC in high school, and he encouraged me to learn as much as I could about alternative regimens during my employment there.

Pam sat in the lounge for hours crying because she didn't want to face Steven in his condition. The reality of what I was dealing with didn't help her emotionally, and I had to leave her alone crying because it was not a time for me to fall apart. The nurses were prepping me for every stage of a slow death, because Steven was standing at the door. The booklet written by the family of Karen Ann Quinlan was an incredibly helpful tool in recognizing the end stages of the death process.

Steven told me he didn't want me to visit him over the weekend because his sisters were coming and he wanted to spend time with them alone. I had made an agreement with myself to say yes to whatever Steven wanted. With only days to live, he was running the show.

It is never easy to make arrangements for the one you love to die. Even when you know the day is coming, picking up that phone to call the undertaker is a laborious undertaking. I did so at the urging of the nurses, who were asking who would handle the body. Steven wanted to be cremated. I wanted to comply with his wish, but I did not agree with cremation.

Hospice nurses are pure angels; they care not only for the dying patient but also for the family. They walked me through everything. Before I left each day, they told me what to expect the next—and they were right. I wondered what helped *them* as they dealt with death every day. Lots of prayer, no doubt.

Pam, Sloopy, and I had a pajama huddle every night during their visit. Pam was the chef, and Sloopy provided the much-needed comic relief. They fed me fantastic meals and food for my soul. They scratched my dandruff, washed my hair, gave me a facial, manicure, and pedicure, and talked about me—as only your good girlfriends can—

for letting myself fall apart. And just like a mother caring for a sick child, they tucked me into bed at a decent hour for a good night's sleep.

I felt refueled and recharged by the time I dropped them at the Allentown airport at 5 A.M. Then I swung by the hospice before heading to the city for work.

Steven was no longer speaking. The doctor said that his vocal cords had been arrested by lesions from the sarcoma. Very glassy-eyed and making motions with his hands, he was being fed intravenously. The nurses said he would probably die within the next forty-eight hours.

I scooped up Steven real close and held him for a long time. I told him I loved him and that I would be back that evening. He grunted and stroked my hair. I laid him back down, and we did our pointer high-five before leaving.

I ran out of that place thinking, *Hold on, Steven, because Mommie and Bo Daddy are back in two days.*

I sped forty minutes from Allentown back to the Poconos, getting there just in time to board the bus to the city. On Tyger's last visit, she'd supplied me with a bagful of taped sermons from her brother-in-law, Bishop Trotter. It seemed that Bishop was ministering directly to me. There was one tape called "Lord, I Need a Jump!" He made an analogy between needing a jump in a car and needing a jump from Jesus. I would have my arm all out of the window praising on that one! It was my favorite.

I had accomplished a major coup at work by garnering the cover of *Vibe* magazine for the Notorious B.I.G., a.k.a. Biggie, a.k.a. Biggie Smalls, and his wife, Faith Evans. The shoot was on the waterfront underneath the Brooklyn Bridge. *Vibe* chose as a setting a vintage black convertible, in which Faith and Biggie were dressed like a gangster and his girl sitting in the backseat.

It was a ninety-plus-degree July day in the city, and there was not an ounce of cool relief for us in the sunshine, not even next to the water.

I had to do a lot of running around for that particular shoot, so I had reserved a car service for the day. My favorite drivers, brothers Nir and Jay, lived just across the water near me in New Jersey, and I always requested them when going home late nights or for early-morning pickups. I checked in with the hospital, and the nurse told me that Steven was definitely going to make his transition soon.

"When are you coming?" she asked, concerned that I wasn't there already. I had asked God to keep me from being there when it happened, and I knew my request would be granted.

"I'll be there this evening after work," I assured her. "Feel free to call me on the following number to keep me posted."

I gave her the number for Nir's car phone. In 1995, we weren't surgically attached to cell phones. They were very expensive back then, and car phones were more accessible and affordable.

The photo shoot was sailing smoothly, while Faith and Biggie were eating up the opportunity to finally show the industry they were a bona fide couple who had weathered a stormy marriage. Meanwhile, the nurse was calling me with an update every hour.

"His breathing is shallow," she said. "What time will you be here?"

I answered, "After work this evening."

"His pupils are dilating," she said the next time she called. "What time will you be here?"

"After work."

"He's starting to lose his grip," she said the next hour. "What time will you be here?"

"After work."

Her calls went on like this all day long. With those up-to-the-minute reports of his demise, I felt as if I were there in the room. Like the kids say, it was TMI—too much information. I couldn't deal anymore. I thanked God I was not in the office trying to handle the reality of my husband's last day alive. A photo shoot was fast-paced action that required my attention, and I was thankful for just the right diversion.

During our lunch break at around three, Biggie took me aside.

"How you doin'?" he quizzed me, genuinely concerned.

I furrowed my eyebrows because I'd never seen him so tender. "I'm good."

"No, you not," he said. "I know what's going on with you. I see you been cryin'. I see you runnin' back and forth to the phone in the car. How's your husband?"

I could only shake my head, and a tear popped out. He scooped me up in a bear hug and rocked me.

"Listen, go home and take care of your business," he said. "This is almost over here."

"No, it's only half over. I have to make sure—"

"I promise, I won't embarrass you," he said with a smile, cutting me off and knowing why I was monitoring his every move. Biggie had a history of going off at photo shoots, screaming that he wouldn't do this or that, and then summoning me to put out the fires.

"I worked hard to get this cover, Biggie. You better not embarrass me, or you'll never have another one," I warned him.

Ah, the power of a publicist: whatever you can do . . . you can un-do.

"I won't, cuz I wants me another cover. You go on to the hospital," he said, kissing me on my forehead and turning me toward the car with a little shove. I didn't even look back. It wouldn't have mattered, because I couldn't see a thing for the tears.

Nir wasn't ready to get off work for the day, so he drop-switched me with his brother Jay, and I advised the hospital that I was on my way. The nurse sighed in relief, but I was a nervous wreck inside, praying for peace to calm my chattering teeth.

God, in His honoring of my prayer, created the most monstrous traffic jam, and it took us more than three hours to make the ninety-minute trek to the Poconos. I had decided to spend the night at the hospital, but I had Jay drop me off home first because I needed clothes for another huge photo shoot with Deborah Cox the next day. And I hadn't made arrangements for the dogs to be fed.

I got my car at the park-and-ride and drove myself to

Allentown. Within twenty minutes, I ran into crawling traffic. The radio said there was an overturned tractor trailer in the direction I was headed. To avoid the traffic, I ducked off at the next exit and took backroads that I had heard of but had never traveled all the way to Allentown.

I was singing, "We have come this far by faith." At the hospice, when the elevator doors opened, the nurse was standing there. She looked at the clock, which read 10:22. She looked at me carrying my clothes and asked, "Didn't you speak to the doctor?"

"No, I've been caught up in traffic everywhere for the last five hours."

"Well, he called you to let you know that Steven died at 9:05."

"He did?" I asked in disbelief.

You know it's going to happen. You're told it will happen. But when it does happen, it's like a karate kick to your stomach by a black belt who's really angry with you.

She helped me off of the elevator and took my overnight bag.

"He wasn't alone," she assured me. "I was with him."

"You were? Thank you," I managed to say.

God had definitely orchestrated the day. Created traffic like none I'd ever seen, caused a diversion at work, and honored my prayer, *Please don't let me be there when he dies.*

"May I use the phone?" I asked.

She seated me at the nurses' station.

"Wouldn't you like to go in to spend some time with him before you start making calls?" she asked.

"No."

She knelt in front of me. "You should go in so that you will have closure."

"No."

"If you don't go, you may regret never having said good-bye," she said.

"Miss, I have been saying good-byes for the last two years," I told her. "We had our good-byes again this morning. I choose to remember him like I saw him last. I don't want to see him dead. I don't want that memory."

Another nurse abruptly picked up the phone to call the chaplain. In seconds, a rotund man was kneeling before me, trying to convince me to go into that room.

"All of you, hear me," I said. "Thank you for everything you have done for us both. You are God's angels, for sure. But nothing can make me go into that room. I am at peace with my soul in not seeing him dead."

They all stared at one another. I heard a nurse in the background say to someone else, "She's traumatized."

I snapped my head in her direction. "No, I'm not traumatized. This is an example of how you stand up when you have the peace and the love of Jesus to hold you up. Father, will you pray with me?"

He was now smiling; he understood what I was saying.

"Yes, child," he said, as he prayed a beautiful prayer and my tears flowed freely.

"Amen," we said together.

"May I have Steven's glasses, photos, wallet, and watch from the room, please?" I asked the nurse.

"What about everything else?" she asked.

"If you could throw it away, I'd appreciate it." The priest was holding my hand.

"Thank you, Father. I'll be fine."

"Is there anyone at home?" he asked.

Wow, there was no one at home. Isn't that just like God to fix it so there is no one else around but Him to lean on in your darkest hour?

I shook my head no and asked, "Is it okay if I make several phone calls?"

The nurse pushed a phone in my direction. My first call was to Steven's sisters, who said they'd meet me at home. Mommie and Bo Daddy said they'd leave first thing in the morning. My senior publicity director at work, Jackie, told me to handle my business at home and she'd handle my work responsibilities.

The nurse brought the things I requested from Steven's room and made one last attempt to get me to see him. After refusing by thanking each of them for their compassion and care, I left exactly the way I came that evening— singing, "We have come this far by faith."

That was July 19, 1995.

CHAPTER EIGHT

The Laying to Rest

Come unto me, all ye that labour and are heavy laden,
and I will give you rest. Take my yoke upon you, and learn of
me; for I am meek and lowly in heart: and ye shall find rest
unto your souls for my yoke is easy and my burden is light.

— MATTHEW 11:28–30

I got in my car after learning my husband had died after a two-year battle with AIDS, and it was an eerie feeling to know that he was gone. For real, forever. I was drained physically, as if someone had literally sucked the life out of me. As soon as I started the car my tape blared "Lord, I Need a Jump!" Did I ever!

I contacted my neighbors, the Parkins family, and had them get their two kids, Jelani and Gyasi, whom I called my sons, ready so they could enter the house with me. I had a funny feeling about going into the house by myself the first time.

Jelani set up a video and walked the dogs, while in the bedroom Gyasi helped me toss out all of the sick-care items, immediately. I went on a cleaning frenzy. By the time we were finished, it looked like a sick person had never been in the house. I guess it was just busywork, but I needed to keep occupied until Steven's sisters arrived.

The next day, we went to the mortician's office to finalize the cremation, and no one made a move to pay for the expense but me. It was settled that the sisters would keep his ashes next to Mama Mo's at their house.

For the funeral, we all decided to wear white. George was on the program to play saxophone, but his mother suffered a stroke the morning of the funeral and he couldn't come. Steven had made special requests for singers and speakers at his service, and everyone complied.

Bishop Sam spoke. "I remember when LaJoyce met Steven. *Every*thing was, 'Steven said,' 'Steven bought,' 'Steven gave!' 'Steven,' 'Steven,' 'Steven!' " he said, mimicking my voice. Everyone roared with laughter.

My friend Arlene sang Steven's favorite song by BeBe and CeCe Winans, "Don't Cry for Me," a cappella, and there wasn't a dry eye in the place.

Pastor K.P. told the truth about Steven being grumpy on the days he cared for him. "We had good times and not so good times," he said honestly.

The eulogy was delivered by a new pastor at Steven's Lutheran home church, so it was important that those who knew him spoke to paint a real picture of the Steven we all knew.

After the service, I was relieved not to attend a burial. We had the repast at his sisters' house, and it was there that I buried Steven and the last bit of the relationship I had with them. Leaving his ashes there was just like putting him in the ground to me. I knew that if I did not take the initiative in maintaining a relationship with his sisters, we wouldn't have one. I had done enough, and my vow was to Steven, not to his sisters. When I hugged them good-bye, I knew that would be the last time I'd see them. My good-bye was sincere, firm, and final.

Those from his side of the family with whom I did choose to maintain a relationship were Uncle Charles and Aunt Peggy and their kids, Kathy, Fabia, and Charles Jr. To this day, we still call one another family.

I had taken a week off from work to handle the aftermath of laying my husband to rest. Bright and early Monday morning I dressed, ready to handle business in town.

Mommie saw me walking out the door. "Where are you going this time of morning?" she asked.

"I'll be back this evening," I said, holding a briefcase full of death certificates and all of the pertinent papers I needed to run my life and my household.

I went all over town, and when I returned I was once again legally LaJoyce Celeste Hunter on everything. Throwing my driver's license on the table for display, I announced that I was back!

Bo Daddy had only one concern: "What you going to do with all this house?"

"I plan to *live* in it," I said. "Steven had better credit, with all those credit cards, and even though I had no credit history, I had the cash. This here is *my* house."

I spent a lot of time that week sleeping, especially after Mommie and Bo Daddy left. I knew that was a sign of grieving. In the middle of my grieving period, Steven's older sister called to ask that I sign over a property in Queens via a quitclaim deed.

"Why do you need my signature at all?" I asked.

"Well, when Steven was in the hospital last time, we FedExed the papers to him so they could be signed and notarized," she explained. "Now all you have to do is sign the deed, because the notary stamped it but forgot to sign it, so it is not valid."

Her call was the first I had heard of all this.

"Oh, really," I said. "Well, that's what you all get for sneaking. It seems that you all are just busy sneaking and lying all the time. If you would have asked me in the first place to get it done, it would have been done right. Since you didn't, I'm not signing anything!"

And that was the last time we spoke on the phone.

Through Catholic Services I found a grief-counseling group that met once weekly. After the first meeting, I understood how important it was to let go of things that I was holding on to, like clothes and photos. That made so much sense to me. Clean out the closet. I called Stacey, Uncle Charles, and Charles Jr. over to have their pick before it all went to the community outreach center and Goodwill.

I sat on the floor in a corner and cried as they tried on the very expensive clothes that had once brought Steven so much joy. Claudette acknowledged how hard it must be for me to get rid of such personal items. I needed them *all* gone. It was a cleansing and a purging that was necessary to move forward from my place of pain. I had to regain my personal power—and fast. The only way to do that was to rest in Jesus.

It took me a while to sort through the photos of us on display all over the house. I knew definitely that those had to go. No way did I want my dead husband staring at me from anywhere. I made separate pouches for all family members and for Godmother Martha, too. They included photos from the wedding until the last time we ever took pictures.

At work, I knocked on Jackie's door. "Have you got a minute?" I asked. "I want you to see something."

I pulled out all the photos and she smiled at them. Jackie was one of the industry-ites Steven had snuggled up to and loved dearly. All of us felt that way about Jackie. I had known her since the 1980s, upon my arrival in New York City, and she was always like a big sister to me. She had called me to get the job at Arista, for which she had referred me. It was during that moment of reminiscence that I got the courage to tell her the truth about Steven's illness. She burst into tears and pushed the photos to the floor.

I went around to her side of the desk to comfort her. Jackie is not the crying type, but this hurt her deeply.

"I promise you, I'm okay," I said. "I promise you, I'm negative."

I knew this was a story I was going to have to tell over and over again, but telling it was necessary for *my* healing.

I understood Steven's sisters' desire to maintain his privacy while he was alive, but it made not an ounce of sense for me to continue to maintain the privacy of a dead man.

I sort of went on a mission after that. I started making lunch, dinner, and weekend dates with people who had been incredibly supportive of me, hoping to find the right time to tell them the truth. The news rocked every single person in the same manner.

I even went on a little crusade and tried to dig up the women with whom he told me he had been intimate. I found out he had had sex with only one friend of Claudette's. The women were thankful I had called at all, but they denied having sexual relations with him.

"Girl, no woman is gonna admit having slept with your dead husband that you are calling to tell them had AIDS!" Claudette said of my crusade.

See, that's the thing about discernment. If you choose to pay attention to it—there it is, staring you in the face. But if you don't pay attention, there you are standing in the back of the church decked out in your wedding gown, admitting to your daddy you shouldn't be getting married . . . and you do it *any*way.

My knowledge about Steven was building, and I was no longer ignoring what was right before me. In spite of my 20/20 vision I had been blinded for a long time, and now I was ready to see some things. I saw that these women were even indignant at the suggestion that they had had sex with him.

Hmmm, even after his death, I'm still uncovering the

truth, I thought. Then it hit me: If he wasn't being promiscuous with these women, was he tipping around on the down low with men? *Oh, my goodness!* There it was!!!!! That's how he got infected! It was then evident that the spiral of lies was spinning deeper and deeper. The web of deception was unraveling. I had a lot of time to think and to piece together the mystery of what had then become the story of my own life.

I began to unweave the complications of our relationship from the beginning, starting with Steven's behavior patterns:

- Lying about having bleeding ulcers, and never taking one medication to treat them
- Having a T-cell count of four, proving that he had to have had the disease at least ten years prior to meeting me
- Probably infecting his first wife, Darlene (who died of AIDS in 1999, four years after Steven)
- Disappearing acts with male friends, especially two in particular whenever they came to town
- Faking promiscuousness with women
- Coming into my life like Prince Charming and sweeping me off of my feet
- Proposing very quickly, then marrying within one year
- Dr. Jekyll and Mr. Hyde behavior
- Monopolizing all of my time
- Sabotaging relationships with friends
- Eavesdropping on my phone conversations with others

- Whining constantly to get his way
- Being a willing giver of oral sex but never wanting to receive
- Wanting certain bedroom favors that I now know to be proclivities of gay men
- Being a virulent homophobe
- Spending money like there was an endless well to dip into (probably because he knew he was going to die)
- Being preoccupied with death, not seeming to mind doing things that could get him killed
- Being verbally abusive
- Not wanting me to go anywhere without him

These are the behavior patterns of a man who harbors a deadly secret, be it down low, AIDS, or both.

Everyone basically wanted to know the same thing: how did I keep it together? My answer is, only by the grace of God. See, that's when you know it's God, because you should be out of your mind and you're not out of your mind. I had resolve, because in my heart Steven was fully forgiven. What he did was all so pedestrian, common, dirty, and cruel—mostly just cruel. After reviewing the scenario in its totality, I understand that Steven was a narcissist and a sociopath. Everything he did, in every way, pointed to it being all about him.

It really is criminal to intentionally do harm. To do that, he had to consider me a nonentity. He made a conscious effort to be passive-aggressive, and it is this behavior that allows HIV/AIDS to proliferate. Unfortunately, his attitude is not unique. It is the main reason why the number of infections is staggering today.

I was spared by the Blood of Jesus from becoming a statistic. I endured what I did in order to fulfill what God planted inside of me, which has to do with the salvation of the world. I carry faith because the Bible says that "to each one, God has given a measure of faith." I have learned to be faithful to what God said in the little stuff, because it is not faith for the stuff, but faith for the journey. Ultimately, it is faith that excites God.

This journey did not rob me of my faith, but definitely put it under fire.

CHAPTER NINE

The Restoration of Love

A new commandment I give unto you, that you love
one another; as I have loved you, that ye also love one another.
By this shall all men know that you are my disciples,
if you have love one to another.

—JOHN 13:34–35

My mother was really worried about my lack of socialization after so many months. She would ask me every Friday with expectation, "What are you doing this weekend?"

"Not a thing," was my standard reply.

Throughout the week, I was running like a crazy woman all around the country, working with Arista artists and attending various functions. I needed the weekend to replenish, and it had nothing to do with Steven, I would tell my mother. But my mother wasn't buying that a bit.

I knew inside that I didn't want to continue on my journey in life alone. I knew that eventually I wanted to go out, have some fun, and maybe even date, but this time I was going to wait. Wait on the Lord. I asked God to help make me ready for the man of God that He wanted me to have.

I understood very clearly that I also had to take responsibility for my actions in the Steven debacle. My actions included a lie. Go back to the first page of Chapter One, when I premeditated a sick day. In case this issue confuses you, I told a lie. We have got to stop saying we fell into sin. You don't fall into sin—you plan it. I *planned* to take a sick day when I was not sick. Had I not planned that sick day, I would have shown up at my part-time teaching job in my typical entertainment industry outfit: a casual black something or other and a ponytail. Steven, in his incessant need to have a vision of perfection by his side, would probably never have looked my way. But having taken off, feigning sickness, I had the time to get all dolled-up, with black leather pants, a red silk blouse, and a headful of freshly blow-dried, bouncing, and behaving hair that drew me right to the enemy.

As I mentioned, the Bible is very clear on this subject in Proverbs 18:22: "*He* who finds a good *wife* finds a good thing." I found Steven. He didn't find me. Yes, when we met, there were fireworks between us. But I didn't have to place my stake in him and make the declaration to all of my friends: "That's gonna be my husband!"

I then proceeded to whip it on him good, adding log after log onto the fire to garner a marriage proposal. He may have had an agenda, but I had one, too.

Once the wedding date was locked, I spent a lot of

time consumed by the planning of *my* wedding. God was putting things right in front of me in plain view, and if I had not been so busy coordinating the wedding like it was another one of my events, maybe I would have seen some of the signs. But at age twenty-eight, when all of your friends have already walked down the aisle and you've got a closet full of bridesmaids' dresses, you look the other way at a lot of things. Compromise is the pen that writes the story of future destruction.

Don't do it! When someone shows you who they are, believe them!

Back in 1990, a girl didn't need to ask the questions that you'd better ask today, such as "Have you ever had a homosexual experience?" And "Have you taken the AIDS test?" And "What's your status?" I didn't adopt the very important concept of NO TEST, NO TOUCH! and NO COVENANT, NO COOCHIE! Yes, doing what your mama told you—save yourself for marriage—is *still* good advice.

While I don't have concrete proof of Steven being on the down low—like catching him in bed with another man—I have the compilation of lies and behavior patterns I discussed earlier.

HIV is not some disease that sneaks up on you. Steven was in denial to the nth degree, and last I checked, the Nile is a river in Egypt. It is time that denial let our people go!

The bottom line in this is my responsibility. I didn't ask enough questions. I wasn't educated enough to get *myself* tested, and I didn't seek God. Matthew 6:33 says, "But seek ye first the kingdom of God and His righteousness and all things shall be added unto you."

In the words of the early departed Biggie, "If you don't know—now you know."

I only share my story so you know what to look out for. Don't make it *your* story and risk becoming a statistic. Now *you* know.

As bad as things had gotten, I knew God was still God. You cannot conquer what you do not confront. I also knew that I could not just sweep my mess under the Cross. I serve the one true master who helped me to overcome all, but I first had to face Him. It made no sense to me to murmur and complain about my situation. The test was not to see what I was going to do. God already knew what I would do. But God's grace is the test to show us where we are in Him.

Some people have gone so far as to say that Jesus had forsaken me—and maybe for a moment in my disobedience, He had. As I said, delayed obedience is still disobedience. During my wilderness experience, God was arranging some things. Only when He was ready did He bring me back onto the scene with a fresh anointing that could not be denied if, this time, I did what *He* ordained. Before an anointing, there is always a crushing, and after a breaking, there is always a blessing. . . .

Christmas 1995
I arrived in Chicago with an airtight calendar that I intended to follow. I had arranged to visit with Gus after

Mommie, Sloopy, and I went to see *Waiting to Exhale*. At work, I had slaved over the publicity details of the movie's soundtrack, and I was excited to sit in an audience to hear the raw public response. We whooped and hollered through the movie and talked back to the screen as only a black audience can do. The afternoon out was soothing to my soul. It was good to be home.

At the Brookshire house, I found Gus had waited for me all day because he didn't know what time I was going to arrive. Mama Brookshire had a fabulous meal on the stove, and I sopped up string bean juice with my corn bread while Tony, Gus's teenage son, serenaded us, trying to convince me that he was the next Usher. I made him sing "Silent Night" and "Twinkle, Twinkle Little Star." I wanted to hear *Tony* sing, not Usher. It turns out that he wasn't such a bad singer. He was a tall, good-looking teen and very well mannered. *Reminds me of Gus at that age,* I thought.

Gus came back to my parents' house and helped me do all the cake and pie baking, as I am the official dessert-maker. At the family gatherings all of my life, I'd be watching my Grannie and aunts cook. No one else in the family knew how to make my Grannie's famous three-layer coconut cake with pineapple filling.

Gus helped me, all right—by licking the spoons! We had not had a marathon conversation since the spring, when he was in truck-driving school, so we were overdue. I discovered his divorce had been finalized July 15. We were amazed that our marital situations had both concluded during the same week.

"You've hugged everyone today except me," Gus pointed out. "Come give me a hug."

Gus was the best hugger in the world. It took only five minutes for us to be fully in love again, and before he left we were kissing on the steps just like when I was sixteen—with him standing one step below me so we could be eye to eye. It was a magical moment, like taking a powerful youth pill.

On Christmas Eve, I went to a church program at Liberty Temple with Darlyn, my best friend from junior high school. Her pastor, Apostle Clifford Turner (who is now her husband), was totally awesome. She and I kept nudging each other, as his message was obviously for us both.

"I need you to drop me off," I told her.

Recognizing the house, Darlyn said, "If you and Gus get back together, I'm going to just pass out!"

With a giggle I said, "Pass out, baby!" and I kissed her Merry Christmas. She was so happy I could hear her praising God right there in the car.

Gus and I attended a midnight Christmas Eve service at St. Albie's, a church in our neighborhood that used to have dances every Saturday night when we were teens—dances that I could never attend, by the way. Gus would go and call me from the phone booth and talk to me for the duration of the dance.

Before the service, he took me to that phone booth and showed me where he had carved out "Gus + LaJoyce" way up high.

A friend of mine asked me if I ever thought that God

would hook me up with the man of my past, to be the man of my future and my present. I had to think about that question and honestly say no. I promised God that the next time, I'd follow *His* leading. LaJoyce's leading was *all* wrong! I did ask that whomever He sent be a man of valor and one who could be the bishop of our household. I also needed the man to have an understanding of me. With all I'd experienced, we would have to connect spirit-to-spirit, because I had become an extremely complex individual.

Gus was definitely like-minded and like-spirited. He followed the Bible in all matters. At six feet four, he was as rock-solid in stature as he was in his faith. He, too, had a serious wound from his marriage that would take time to heal. Together, as boyfriend and girlfriend, we would heal by seeking and serving the Lord.

"What are you doing for New Year's?" I asked him one night while he was massaging my scalp.

"What do you want me to do?" he answered.

"Would you like to come to New York? We can go to the Kirk Franklin concert at the Apollo and then Watch Night Service at church."

"That sounds great," Gus said.

My mother was a travel agent in her retirement, and she loved planning cruises. She didn't like being troubled with writing airline tickets, but that didn't stop me from asking her.

"Mommieeee!" I screamed happily through the house from the upstairs den. "Gus wants to come to New York for New Year's!"

She appeared at the top of the stairwell. "Oh really! When can you leave? When do you want to come back?"

"I'm flexible," Gus admitted. He was home in Chicago working with his uncle's rehab business. He was recovering from an experience with his truck when it met black ice on a Colorado mountain.

"When that truck started to slide out of control toward a railing with nothing but mountains below it," he remembered, "I just let go of the wheel and screamed, 'Jesus!' And it came to a complete stop."

I had my hand over my mouth in disbelief. But isn't that just like Jesus? When you call on Him—He'll come.

So, Gus was officially retired from truck driving, making him available to visit with me in New York. When my mother came back to the den, she had booked and paid for Gus's ticket for a four-day stay. She was as happy as she could be seeing us together. So was I.

During Christmas we decided that we would not be having any sex. "We're going to save that for when we get married," Gus advised me.

"Married?" I asked, with an eyebrow raised. I wondered wherever he got such an idea. I didn't dare ask, because we planned it all out with each other between ages twelve and seventeen. We had even mapped out our kids' names back when we were young. We wanted six children.

"Yep, married. We're going to do everything God's way so our relationship will be blessed," he said.

I did not argue with that wish, not one bit.

On the day Gus arrived in New York, I had an Arista car service pick him up from the airport. He said he nearly fell out when he saw the man standing there with a sign reading BROOKSHIRE. When he reached my office, my buddy Johnny took him for a walking tour of Manhattan until I got off work.

When we got home, Gus stood in the foyer with his coat on while I ran around turning on the lights, lighting the wood-burning stove, making sure the coal stove in the basement was filled, and introducing him to the dogs, who sniffed him completely.

"Take off your coat," I said every time I passed him.

As I whizzed by him for the tenth time, he caught me by the arm and asked, looking around, "How much are your expenses a month?"

"Twenty-three hundred dollars," I answered. "Why?"

"I can do that." He then took off his coat.

I thought, *That was cute, he wanted to make sure he could handle my lifestyle before he got comfortable. Mama and Daddy Brookshire sure raised him right.*

Our night in the city for the concert was a blast on the night before New Year's Eve. The city was still filled with the spirit of Christmas. Bishop Sam was the emcee for the concert, and I took Gus backstage to meet him. He was totally protective of me by this point of my life, as he had been with me through a fiancé in the 1980s, a marriage, a death, and AIDS. Bishop Sam talked to Gus a really long time before announcing joyfully, "Okay, daughter, I approve."

After the concert we all went to Wells Restaurant for chicken and waffles, jazz music, and lots of laughter. We got back to the Poconos just as the sun was rising.

On New Year's Eve, I fed Gus breakfast in bed.

"So you're treating me like a king," he said.

"I'm not doing anything for you now that I wouldn't continue to do for you," I said. "Don't start it if you can't finish it, as Mommie would say." Gus laughed out loud. He'd been around my family long enough to know the Mommie-isms by which I governed my life.

When we walked into Watch Night Service at church that evening, every eye was on Gus. He is strikingly handsome (in my opinion) and imposing in stature. And he is as gentlemanly as he is good-looking—taking off my coat, allowing me to get seated first, taking the aisle seat. It was all noticed by my church family. There were so many audible collective *mmmm*'s from the members that Gus and I exchanged glances. *Here we go*, I thought.

During 1996 we talked so much on the phone that our bills were outrageous! I told him that I would rather use that money for a plane ticket. He agreed because he was even more of a money-miser than I was, in part due to his mathematical mind. He can figure out numbers in his head while I'm still trying to punch them into a calculator! So once a month I went to Chicago or he came to visit me. My folks were thrilled seeing me so often. Although they knew I came to spend those weekends with Gus, they were happy just seeing me happy.

We also started the art of love-letter writing. When we

were teenagers, we would write each other from our summer vacation spots. Gus called my writings "The Strawberry Letters" because they were written on stationery with pictures of strawberries on it. The Brothers Johnson also had a record called "Strawberry Letter 23," which became our favorite song from 1976 and on.

Gus's letters were deep and very romantic. He was writing me stuff like ". . . The plan is to love you long, deep and forever. And for that, you can hold me accountable. . . ."

Whaaaaaaat!!!! I screamed out loud. I would try to one-up him in my letters, but he'd come back with something ten times better. There was a letter in my mailbox every other day. To me, the letters were better than the phone calls. Gus, like me, journaled daily and was a profound thinker. So the letters were a flashlight into the windows of his soul.

"Good night, sweetie," he said on the phone one Wednesday night. "I've got an early morning, so I'll talk to you later."

The next morning he called to wake me up, and fifteen minutes later he was ringing my doorbell. "But you called me from home and said good night," I said, hugging him.

"Nope, I was in Ohio."

"You drove all night?!!"

"Yes, I did, and it was worth it to surprise you," he said, sealing the surprise in kisses.

Realizing the time, I said, "You have a choice. I can stay home today or stay home tomorrow."

"Stay home tomorrow, it's Friday," he said, yawning. "I'll get some sleep."

I bounced off to work completely energized, happy, and grateful.

In June, I had received a promotional kit at work for an artist-development workshop run by members from the R&B group Ray, Goodman & Brown. It was an intensive course called "So You Wanna Be a Star." I sent the package to Gus because Tony and his cousin Darren talked of nothing but becoming singing stars. I kept trying to tell Gus to tell them both that if they were really serious, they had to do their homework to perfect the craft. I asked Gus to send the boys for the summer so they could attend the class.

Not only did the boys come, but Gus took off work for two months so he could chaperone them into and out of the city. The house was alive with the boom-boom-boom of teenage boys' feet, conversations shouted from room to room, and the aroma of good food.

When they arrived, I served them smothered potatoes and onions, sautéed apples, turkey sausage, grits with cheese, and homemade biscuits. Over breakfast the next day we had a house meeting. I told my three new male roommates that I don't like no messy house, no pee on the toilet seats or floor, and no jelly or toast crumbs in my butter. We divvied up the household chores, and I gave seventeen-year-old Darren the keys to my new Honda Civic to drive. The boys were in hog heaven.

Tony and Darren got jobs in town at Burger King. Making money was nice, but it could not interfere with their class. Chris Curry from Ray, Goodman & Brown was very impressed with the dedication and the development of the boys. I felt like the proud mama of them both.

Tony always felt like he was my kid, too. He was born my senior year, in 1980, after Gus and I had had one of our annual breakups. This breakup seemed final, though, because I was not ready to have sex and Gus, being a year older and with raging teenage hormones, was.

"I don't want to get pregnant," I told him.

"You won't get pregnant," he countered.

"How do you know?" I asked.

" 'Cause you won't," was all he could say.

"No, I can't. I'm not ready for all of that. But you go ahead and I'll look the other way," I suggested.

"There's no way I'm going to disrespect you," he said. "We've got to break up."

I was crushed. Six months later Gus wanted to get back together. Of course we did, but not without his admission that there was going to be a baby.

It took everything I had not to say, "See?" I couldn't do that because I was the first person he told. Gus and I had been best friends long before we were girlfriend and boyfriend. We often told each other things that, to this day, we've told no one else.

So Tony felt like mine, and I treated him like mine.

Part of the boys' training was a real-life experience in the music business. I took them to work with me to attend a press day for Donell Jones and a video shoot for the Bad Boy Records R&B male group 112.

"Today will be action-packed," I warned them before leaving home. Gus came along, too, figuring it would be fun. I laid down a few ground rules: "There will be no acting starstruck. No photo taking until the appropriate time. No sleeping. Pay attention. Help out when you're asked. Otherwise stay out of the way. Look interested. You are on assignment, so act like it."

They all agreed to the terms. "One last thing: Don't embarrass me, or I'll kill you."

With Donell Jones, we hit many press outlets, including syndicated radio shows and television appearances, before lunch. By the time we made our way to Sylvia's Restaurant in Harlem, Gus and the boys were exhausted. I was relentless in trying to show them a day in the life of a star *and* a publicist, and I wouldn't let them close their eyes for a second.

I caught Gus dozing off in the limo. "Oh, no you don't," I admonished him. "You think I have fun doing all of this?"

"No, you wanna be a star," I would say, nudging Tony and Darren awake. "If Donell is not sleeping, y'all can't sleep!"

Laughing, Donell interjected, "I want to, but she won't let me."

The video shoot took place that evening in Times Square, directly in front of the building where the ball is dropped on New Year's Eve. Total and The Notorious B.I.G. were also featured in the video. All of the Bad Boy acts were on the artist roster I handled at Arista, and I loved my little artists to death. They had been through a lot with me, and they were so happy to finally meet Gus.

By the end of the shoot, around midnight, we were all wiped out. But the boys were then certain that being a star was what they wanted.

To celebrate the boys' graduation from their class, we gave them a party where the guests had to demonstrate their talent. It was a blow-out! We had a snow cone machine, a hot dog machine, a nacho maker, and all sorts of goodies.

Darren showed off his abilities by singing the Donell Jones hit "Knocks Me Off My Feet," with Gus, Tony, and I singing backup.

Gus serenaded me with an oldie but goodie that is a Chicago favorite. "You and I have an understanding . . . ," he crooned. Everyone screamed and clapped and cried at the very open display of Gus's love for me. I cried, too, because I was beginning to feel the anxiety of separation from my boys and my boyfriend, since it was almost time for school to begin.

Tony took a stand. "I want to stay here and go to school. I don't want to go back to Chicago," he pleaded. "I don't care what you all are doing with your relationship. I just want to stay. Can't I stay?"

"Of course," I said immediately.

"We'll see," Gus said in a what-are-you-gonna-do-with-a-fifteen-year-old-high-school-sophomore tone.

Gus and I were so busy over the summer working on the boys' development as singers that we didn't lock down a specific date for our marriage. After hours of talking and planning, we decided that Darren would return home to take his post as drum major of the Chicago Vocational High School Marching Band, and he and Tony would move in.

They were all packed up and ready to pull out to Chicago when Gus knocked on the door and ordered me to get the calendar.

"Our mamas will never let me move in without us having an official wedding date," he said knowingly.

"Riiiiiight," I agreed, running for the calendar.

We decided on April 26, 1997.

The longest two weeks of my life were spent waiting for Gus and Tony to return. We got Tony enrolled at East Stroudsburg High School, and Gus took two jobs as a truck driver—for UPS and for Airborne Express. He killed himself working them both for about two months until he decided which he liked better. He settled in at Airborne.

We took a weekend trip to the city to look for the perfect ring. In the store we had an argument over the size of the ring. Gus had selected the largest ring the store had. It was colossal!

"I can't wear that every day!" I said, thinking of the thugs who were always hanging out with Biggie, Puffy, OutKast, and the other rappers I had to work with daily.

"Why not?" Gus asked, offended.

"Because it's not conducive to my lifestyle of running

around with rappers in the streets of New York City," I said realistically.

"Who said that will always be your lifestyle?" he said, trumping me.

I had to think about that one. I had never thought about a working life without press days, photo shoots, and 250 calls a day. My job was a dream job, but it wasn't completely my dream. Mine was to write books, and Gus knew that—so was his, actually. He was a witness to my getting up daily at four in the morning to write. Now we stood in the jewelry store trying to buy the ring that would celebrate our love, and I was forced to consider the ultimate long-term goal of my professional career.

"A ring is simply supposed to be an ornament to show your love for me," I said, trying to give him a lesson on what engagement rings mean.

"There is no ring in this place big enough to show how much I love you," Gus said loud enough for everybody in the store to hear.

This scene reminded me of another time we had a squabble, and it was over who loved whom more!

Examining the ring he wanted to buy, I thought of the price; it looked like five carats. "Something like this is too expensive," I said, remembering the ring I got from my first husband, payments for which became one of our monthly bills.

Gus fumed. "Don't count my money. I'm paying cash," he said. "I know what you're thinking."

I laughed out loud because only Gus would know that

at that moment I was thinking about how I ended up paying for my own wedding ring the first time around. In that instance Gus made me sick, because he knew what I was thinking next year already. I wasn't walking out of the store with that ring, but I needed to find another way to tell him.

"You know what, honey? It looks like a cocktail ring—something you wear only for special occasions. It doesn't look like a ring to wear every day."

He conceded and picked five stunning rings and had me select three. The salesman said the ring would be ready in a week. So it would be a surprise, Gus made the final selection when I wasn't looking. We left the jewelry store laughing hand in hand because all of the disagreements we'd ever had had been over the measure of our love.

In December of 1996, Gus called me at work to say the ring was ready.

"Do not open the box," he ordered knowingly.

"I wouldn't do that. . . ."

"Mmmmm, okay," he said, laughing. "Leave the box on the counter."

When Gus got home from work that night, he woke me from a deep sleep and asked for my hand in marriage. On bended knee, wearing a tuxedo shirt and bow tie, he presented me with a whopper four-carat pear-shaped diamond ring with baguettes. I was screaming and laughing like a little kid.

Our ivory wedding invitation was embossed in gold, with a boy angel kissing a girl angel. It read:

The Beginning of a Harmonious Life
will commence on
Saturday, April twenty-sixth
nineteen hundred and ninety-seven
As I will finally marry my childhood sweetheart
my Soul Mate in Christ
and my first best friend.
Come rejoice and witness the wedding of

LaJoyce Celeste Hunter

and

Gus William Brookshire, Jr.

One o'clock in the afternoon
Reaching Out For Jesus Christian Center
Stroudsburg, Pennsylvania

We invited two hundred guests from everywhere to celebrate our special day. I had the dress, a champagne-colored gown from Nordstrom, shipped to my office to keep there. Gus was seriously trying to break all the rules and get a peek at what I was going to wear.

One day at work during a Black Music meeting, the fire alarm went off. We were so used to the false alarms, no one moved. The office manager came into the conference room out of breath. "Get out of the building! The sixth floor is on fire!"

We all rolled onto Fifty-seventh Street, and word circulated that the fifth floor had been damaged by water as well as by fire. I worked on the fifth floor. *Oh no, my wedding dress*, I thought. I shook that off and looked up into the sky: "Lord, I know ain't no way a burnt wedding dress will happen to me twice." A peace enveloped me in the midst of the madness, and I quietly slipped from the crowd into the Limited Express store next door and went shopping.

When we were allowed to re-enter the building, we learned that the sixth floor was indeed charred and several offices on the fifth floor were waterlogged. But not mine! My office and my dress were untouched. Hallelujah!! I had had the office consecrated with anointed oil and had offered many prayers before I ever stepped foot inside, just like God had instructed me. Now, He was rewarding my obedience. I thought of one of my favorite scriptures: *He who dwells in the secret place of the most high, shall abide under the shadow of the almighty.* "God keeps covering me," I said when I entered my dry office.

In March, just before the wedding, I had to take a ten-day trip to Los Angeles with Biggie to complete publicity for his *Life After Death* album. He would make an appearance on the Soul Train Awards, and there were also several must-attend parties. Biggie had broken his femur in a car accident, so he was walking with a cane. It was decided that the most comfortable mode of transportation for him would be an SUV.

We made the rounds in Los Angeles for lengthy press days. Biggie had a new attitude, and I was happy. Our relationship couldn't continue if the entourages of I-don't-know-how-many folks needed to be accommodated to get *his* business conducted. We had one serious conversation, and Biggie surprisingly put an end to the mess I had endured since our working relationship began. With a lean crew of two in tow, Biggie became the darling of Los Angeles, or so it appeared.

At the Soul Train Awards, the crowd in the rafters booed relentlessly throughout Biggie's acceptance speech. *That's not good,* I thought. The East Coast/West Coast rapper rivalry was supposed to have simmered down.

Deep in my core I knew something bad was going to happen. I decided to leave Los Angeles two days early. I called Gus and told him my calendar indicated I was staying after the awards only to attend two more parties.

"Come on home if you don't want to stay, baby," he said soothingly.

"It just doesn't make any sense to stay for some party. Mommie always said, You've gotta know when to leave the party. And something just doesn't feel right."

I didn't really want to articulate exactly what I was feeling.

"Come on home," Gus reiterated. "It's never right when it doesn't feel right."

I gave Biggie the tickets to the *Vibe* magazine party.

"I'm leaving L.A. early on the first thing smoking," I told him.

"Aw, Ma, don't leave me out here. We're gonna have some fun," Biggie pleaded.

"You need to go on to London like you're scheduled to do," I reminded him.

"I'm having too much fun out here. I'm even thinking

about getting a house. They love me in Cali!" he exclaimed, opening his arms wide.

"No, Big, they *don't* love you. They booed you tonight."

He pooh-poohed me with a wave of his hand.

"I'm done," I said. "Can't I go home and get some stuff done for my wedding? I've been here with you eight days taking care of *you*. Can I please get married?"

He gave me a bear hug and asked for my tickets to the *Vibe* party. I left him with a *Los Angeles Times* journalist who was writing a feature article on Biggie that was long overdue.

At four in the morning the next day, Michelle Joyce, Bad Boy's marketing director, called me, screaming, "Thank God, you're safe! Thank God, you're home!"

"Yes, I'm home. MJ, what's wrong?" I asked, trying to calm her frenzy.

"Everyone is looking for you. Turn on CNN. Biggie is dead!"

I freaked!

There on CNN was the truck I had been sitting in for the last eight days. It was all shot up. "Sweet Jesus!" was all I could say. Then I went into a cold shake. Gus held me close for the rest of the night. I couldn't sleep. I kept waking up from nightmares of being in the truck. If I had still been in Los Angeles, no doubt I would have been in the truck with Biggie when he was shot!

God saved me yet again. That bad feeling I had while in Los Angeles? Well . . . this was it. I was shown once again the importance of moving when the Spirit says move.

The delayed obedience on this one could have meant my life.

I took off that Monday from work because I was depressed with a capital D and that recurring nightmare had kept me up all night. I was in no condition to field phone calls, let alone the volume of calls that were bound to be tripled due to Biggie's death. Some people who really cared about me suggested that I was traumatized and advised me to seek counseling. I flipped them off, telling them that God and I would handle this one together, just like always.

My record business mentor, Terri Rossi, finally got through to me, threatening to call Arista's human resources director if I didn't get a counselor over to my office. Reluctantly, I made the call. I knew I needed to, because I was filled with conflicting emotions: elation about my nuptials, which were going to happen in less than four weeks, and sadness at the death of my premier artist, whom I'd raised up from the beginning of his career. Yep, I needed a counselor.

The little woman who came right over was way too perky for my taste. I was crying, falling deeper into depression as she sat there telling me how I *should* feel, when my assistant, Peri, interrupted to say that Marie Brown was on the phone.

Miss Marie was my literary agent who was helping me to, very quietly, get published. Peri was instructed to interrupt me any time she called. I stopped the perky counselor from speaking for a moment while I took the call. What Miss Marie had to say changed my life.

"I know you're busy with Biggie's death and all, but

HarperCollins wants you to write *Soul Food* based on the movie. Have you heard about it?"

"Of course. We're doing the soundtrack," I said, drying my eyes.

"Well, my dear, I've been going back and forth with them for the last couple of weeks over the money, because you deserve it, but you only have five weeks to do it. Can you?"

"Whhhhhhhaaaaat?!!! Of course I can!" I screamed in jubilation. Little Miss Perky was scribbling madly in her notepad. This display of elation after a fit of tears needed to be documented, no doubt. "When do I start?"

Miss Marie calmly stated, "Today, dear. I'll send over everything."

I stood on the side of my desk, did my hallelujah-shout dance, shook Miss Perky's hand good-bye, and slammed the door. I praised in my office for a half hour straight, because right when I was about to walk down a deep tunnel of depression, God said, No! Right at the edge of an ultimate depression, God manifested my ultimate dream.

I thought, *What, was Gus prophetic?* With a marriage and a book, my whole life was about to change.

Bishop Sam married us, and Pastor K.P. conducted the Inclusion Ceremony, in which we married Tony into our union. My Nordstrom gown and gloves were accented by bouquets of calla lilies that my maid of honor, Tyger, and I both carried. Gus was all *GQ'd* up in a suitlike black tuxedo. His lifelong best friend, Phil, was our best man, and

Tony walked me down the aisle. Our parents only needed to sit and enjoy the ceremony.

Gus and I did a lot of crying leading up to the day of the wedding. We would just look at each other and cry tears of joy. Mommie, Bo Daddy, Mama, and Daddy Brookshire were also overjoyed at our union. Daddy Brookshire—blind and all—sat in the front row shouting his approval with Amens.

My longtime friend and former client, R&B crooner Eric Gable, sang the BeBe Winans song "Searching for Love." His rendition was so stirring and Spirit-filled that he got a thunderous round of applause in the middle of the song. Gus and I exchanged glances; his vocals had far surpassed our expectations. Eric set the tone for the rest of the service.

The service concluded with Holy Communion, and we were pronounced man and wife! There are people from our childhood who still can't believe that Gus and I are really married . . . finally. Neither can we.

Because of my friendly relationship with members of the press and the amazing story of our reunion, our wedding was featured in a full-page story in the Vows section of the *New York Times*! We were also in *Jet* magazine, *Sister 2 Sister* magazine, and *The New York Beacon News*. Miss Lucille even gave us another wedding reception at Wells Restaurant in Harlem for those who couldn't make it to the Poconos, and she demanded I wear my gown, to "re-create the moment," she said.

Gus and I did not have any issues with the name

change, because I had been writing "LaJoyce Brookshire" since I was twelve years old. In the back of those diaries Gus gave me for Christmas, I had written the names of the six children we wanted to have. And of course, "LaJoyce Celeste Brookshire" was written in script, print, boldface with a marker, and crayon!

I reclaimed the love of my life by keeping Jesus preeminent in mine. Where Christ is in the center, he holds all things together, as it says in Colossians.

Gus and I enjoyed a deluxe honeymoon at the five-star, all-inclusive Grand Lido Resort in Negril, Jamaica. (Let this be my shameless plug for what we feel to be the most romantic destination on the planet.) Very early every morning I would rise to work on my *Soul Food* manuscript. I was in complete bliss, waking up next to the man I'd loved my whole life and writing books, as I had always wanted to do. It was a true blessing to have both. I remembered what God told me when I could have done something wrong: "I'll bless you." No one but God could have given it to me a hundredfold like what I was experiencing.

While Gus and I don't have the six kids we dreamed of in our teenage years—because we wised up—we are blessed with one amazing little girl, Brooke Angel. We waited three years before praying and actively working toward having a child. Then it took two years more before I became pregnant. In the back of my mind I thought of the little trip to the clinic that I had taken ten years earlier and wondered whether I had fully repented. The pregnancy was proof that I had. This was an awesome blessing for us.

I was ordered to get bed rest and to work only a limited schedule. After doing national book tours for *Soul Food* and *Web of Deception*, I once again settled in with Debra at the National Black Leadership Commission on AIDS in my old post as director of communications. The BLCA staff was overjoyed with the pregnancy, as they had not had a baby on board to spoil in many years.

I had also taken on the task of earning a doctoral degree in naturopathy. I wanted to pursue another lifelong passion, holistic healing. I was living an organic lifestyle that I tried to share with others, but I had no official credibility in the field. Being on a limited work schedule for the baby would give me just the time I needed to complete the courses through a local accelerated-study group.

I was so busy at work trying to get everything in order before early maternity leave at seven months that I defied the doctor's order to stay home every other day. I worked only a four-day week: Monday, Tuesday, and Wednesday in the office, and Thursday at home. My doctor wanted me home on Tuesdays.

"You're going to be forty when you deliver," the doctor warned. "You don't need all of that bumping around on the commuter bus and the bustle of the city every day."

I looked at having a baby at forty as a blessing, not a curse. But everyone in the medical field was looking at me like I was a nut for waiting to have a first baby so late.

Mommie would call me every Tuesday at work and tell me off for being there: "You better not let anything happen to that baby! Why are you even working today?!!"

The first Tuesday that I actually listened to the doctor and stayed home was on 9/11. The events that transpired in New York City that day would have been no place for a pregnant woman. See, God saved me again!!!

That morning I was actually enjoying Harry Belafonte on the *Today* show, marveling at how well he looked for his age and eating oatmeal with sautéed apples and blueberries. Following Harry was some new author. I was looking forward to seeing who would be interviewed, since I had not been able to get the attention of the *Today* show producers in spite of two bestselling books.

The program was interrupted to show the plane hitting the first tower.

"Whaaaat? Are the air-traffic controllers asleep?" I wondered aloud.

When the second plane hit, I pushed my oatmeal bowl away and screamed, "That was no accident!"

Right after the second plane hit, the first call was from my mother.

"You'd better have your behind home today . . ."

The phone started ringing off the hook. Everyone wanted to make sure I was home. The bedlam of people running in the streets was too much for me. I turned off the TV and kept my 11 A.M. hair appointment. Even downtown Stroudsburg, Pennsylvania—ninety minutes away from New York City—had turned into a ghost town. Everyone had canceled their appointment, and I was one of only three people in the salon. While I was there, the news came in about the Pentagon also being hit.

Gus was so exhausted that he kept calling to be certain I wasn't trying to make my way to the city to see if I could help.

"I have this vision of you standing on a street corner with your pregnant self handing out money because that's all you can do," he said, worried.

I was a wreck. I was worried about my friends. The vision of those planes was embedded in my mind. I decided I would not pass on grief to my baby. Two days after the attacks, I had seen all I needed to for a lifetime. I turned off the TV and left a videotape recording that I labeled "For Brooke," and went to Debra's house.

I guess I had a strange look on my face, because she shouted, "Oh my God, what's wrong!"

I started to cry. "I have to be someplace other than my house watching television. I can't take any more."

"C'mon in here, pregnant woman," she ordered. "Hungry?" she asked, then answered: "That's a stupid question. You're pregnant. Sit down. I'll cook."

We did not talk any office talk for an entire day. Debra fed me the best fried fish ever—for hours. We sat on her deck and enjoyed the beauty of the Poconos and wondered if the ugliness of the city would ever disturb the lushness of the vegetation on the mountain that we had come to love.

Those devastating events inspired Gus and me to cling to each other even more, to proclaim our love to each other even more, and to worship God even more.

On Friday, February 1, 2002, at 7:32 A.M., Brooke Angel Brookshire was born by C-section, weighing in at eight pounds, ten ounces, and measuring twenty-one inches. The doctor and nursing staff had marveled at the detailed Birth Plan I had written. A scheduled C-section is a well-coordinated event. The pediatrician knew that he was to administer no vaccinations to the baby, introduce no foreign nipples—as I was going to breast-feed—and use antifungal ointment instead of drops in Brooke's eyes. Gus's job was to follow the baby. Mommie had me covered.

The birthing event had left Gus so emotionally drained that by the time I reached my room he had lost his voice, had blazing red eyes, and was experiencing flu-like symptoms. I sent him home for bed rest at least through the weekend. Our lives would be high octane once I got home.

When I first held Brooke and sang the songs I always sang while pregnant, she stopped crying as if she recognized them. What a miracle God had given to us. And it was only because the Lord had made it possible for me to trust and love again.

> He brought me forth also into a large place;
> He delivered me because he delighted in me. The Lord rewarded me according to my righteousness, according to the cleanness of my hands in his eyesight.
> . . . As for God, his way is perfect. . . ."
> —Psalms 18:24–25

God indeed is perfect. I trusted Him when I was at a terrible crossroads. When I took the time to listen to Him,

He said, "I'll bless you." I'm living that blessing each day with a husband who loves the Lord, and a daughter, too. I am additionally blessed to be HIV-negative and still in the game of life. And I am certain that the only way to play the game of life is with God before you.

Our mission statement in the Brookshire home is:

"Every day in every way, present God's Word as a dying man to dying men, as we seek the Kingdom of God first because *all* things, not just some, but *all* things will be added unto us."

When you seek God, many truths will uncover themselves. When you seek God, you may not be inclined to harbor a horrible secret of your son, your brother, your friend, or your spouse. When you seek God, only the truth will make you free. When you seek God, you will know that secrets are just lies not spoken that can steal, kill, and destroy like the enemy who walks the earth seeking those whom he can devour.

My final thought is one from Bishop Sam, with a little addendum from me: "Wherever you go, whatever you do, and whomever you do it with, if God doesn't give it to you, it's not worth having."

And if I had to say Amen, I think I'd put one right there.

Resources

My people are destroyed for lack of knowledge.

—HOSEA 4:6

Here are the most recent devastating statistics on HIV/AIDS, according to the National Centers for Disease Control and Prevention (CDC) and the Henry J. Kaiser Family Foundation:

As of 2006:

- African-Americans accounted for 51 percent of all HIV infections in the thirty-two states that require reporting.
- African-American women accounted for 67 percent of HIV diagnoses among females in 2005.
- In African-American women, 80 percent of infections were attributed to heterosexual transmission, of which only 17 percent were due to intravenous drug use.
- African-American women accounted for 67 percent of HIV/AIDS cases, Latinas 15 percent, and white women 17 percent.

- In 2005, AIDS was among the leading causes of death for women overall and was the number-one cause of death in black women between the ages of twenty-five and thirty-four—their childbearing years.
- Since the beginning of the epidemic, blacks have accounted for 37 percent of all persons with AIDS.
- Estimated AIDS prevalence among African-Americans is clustered in a handful of states: New York, Florida, California, Texas, Maryland, Georgia, New Jersey, Pennsylvania, Illinois, and Washington, DC—accounting for 72 percent of African-Americans estimated to be living with AIDS in 2005. New York, Florida, and California top the list. These ten states also account for a majority of newly reported AIDS cases of African-Americans—71 percent in 2005.
- African-American teens ages thirteen to nineteen represented 15 percent of all cases; however, they accounted for 65 percent of new AIDS cases reported for teens in 2005.
- A similar impact can be seen in African-American children under the age of thirteen, whose transmissions are most likely perinatal but can also be through sexual contact.
- AIDS was the third leading cause of death for African-Americans ages twenty-five to thirty-four in 2005, compared to the sixth leading cause of death for whites and Latinos in this age group.

Ask Questions and
Avoid Becoming a Statistic

I always tell people that I did not complete my due diligence when I first met Steven. When dating, we are often guilty of taking more time to find the right outfit or buy the right car than we do before jumping in the sack.

Remember how we used to play the game 20 Questions? Well, nowadays we need to play 200 Questions! Audiences at my public appearances have told me they would be challenged to come up with 200 insightful questions to ask.

While some of the following questions may seem rudimentary, they should be asked. And the answer should not be taken for granted just because the person is fine and is paying for you to have a nice dinner. Take the emotion out of the equation and believe what is being presented before you.

Both men and women should ask these questions prayerfully, and when something doesn't seem right, it probably isn't right. If something sounds like a lie, it probably is a lie. Love *your*self enough to walk off before you become enmeshed in a web of deception like I was.

1. Have you been tested for HIV?
2. What is your status?
3. Will you take an HIV test with me?
4. Would you mind if I watch your blood drawn? I don't mind if you watch mine being drawn.
5. Will you allow me to hear your result? I don't mind if you hear mine. (If the answer is no, *run!*)

6. Are you willing to wait to become intimate three months after taking the HIV test to take another test? (This gives you time to actually ask all of these questions and to build a friendship and a relationship. Then, who knows? You may actually find out you really like him or her—or not.)

7. How much time do you think should pass before becoming sexually intimate?

8. How do you feel about abstinence?

9. When was your last intimate encounter?

10. How do you feel about condom use?

11. Are you willing to use a condom? (Remember what I said about trying to combat HIV with a rubber device! *After* you complete your discovery about the person—then and only then—do I recommend a condom as a precautionary measure if you must engage in sex.)

12. When was your last relationship?

13. Are you still searching for your soul mate?

14. Do you believe that there is a soul mate for everyone?

15. Have you ever been in love?

16. When you were younger, did you experience puppy love?

17. Was your last relationship a sexual fling or something serious?

18. What ended the relationship?

19. Do you think men and women can be friends once their relationship is over?

20. Do you believe in having a monogamous relationship?

21. Do you believe in celibacy?

22. Do you date around?
23. Do you believe in casual sex?
24. How many people have you dated at once?
25. Do you think that humans need companionship in order to survive?
26. What do you consider physical intimacy?
27. Have you ever dated interracially?
28. What do you think of interracial dating?
29. Have you dated someone older than you? By how many years?
30. Have you dated someone younger than you? By how many years?
31. In your relationships, do you communicate well?
32. Have you ever had a same-sex encounter?
33. Have you ever kicked it with your boys? (This is new terminology for men who have sex with other men and who refuse to say they are bisexual. Don't ever say *homosexual*, because brothers on the down low feel like *homo* is a dirty word. Ask it boldly, because now you know, too.)
34. If he/she answers yes to the bisexual issue: Are you praying for deliverance and is this a challenge you are trying to overcome?
35. Do you support the homosexual lifestyle?
36. Do you support gay marriages?
37. Are you a Christian?
38. Are you saved?
39. Do you pray?
40. Where do you go to church?
41. Who is Lord of your life? (If you are living a life walking with the Lord Jesus Christ, this is where you and he/she may part company.)

42. How did you choose your religion?
43. What is your greatest testimony?
44. Should everyone have a religious belief?
45. What defines a hypocrite?
46. Do you believe in life after death?
47. If you were to die today, would you enter Heaven or Hell?
48. Do you believe in Heaven and Hell?
49. Are your personal affairs in order?
50. Do you have life insurance?
51. What would people say about you at your funeral?
52. What song do you want sung at your funeral service that defines your life?
53. Has your life been a blessing or a curse?
54. Have you been a blessing to other people?
55. Do you believe in blessing strangers?
56. Do you practice the Golden Rule: Do unto others as you would have others do unto you?
57. Do you believe in karma?
58. Where are you from?
59. How were you raised?
60. Tell me about your family?
61. What kind of relationship do you have with your mother? (This is very important! Hang around for a while to watch this play out. This *is* the telling moment.)
62. What kind of relationship do you have with your father?
63. What did your mother or father always tell you that you found out for yourself to be true?
64. What kind of relationship do you have with your brothers and sisters?

65. Do you have a best friend?

66. What is your definition of a friend?

67. Are you married? (I know this seems very basic, but women and men are entering into relationships with a married person simply because they have never asked. *Ask!*)

68. Have you ever been married?

69. (If yes) What type of relationship do you have with your ex?

70. Why did you get divorced?

71. Did you ever cheat on your spouse?

72. Have you ever hit a woman or a man?

73. Do you think it is okay to hit a woman?

74. Do you have children?

75. (If yes) Are you diligent with your child support?

76. Would you like to have more children?

77. Are you able to have more children?

78. Do you have baby mama drama? (Don't laugh. If you hang around long enough, this will be important to you.)

79. Do you have a pet?

80. Are you happy?

81. What would you do to be happier?

82. Where would you go to be happier?

83. What type of work do you do?

84. Do you enjoy your work?

85. Who is your professional mentor?

86. What do you think is your life's assignment?

87. Do you have any plans to accomplish this assignment?

88. What is your time line?

89. Are you scared or excited about your new plans?

90. Do you have professional guidance in the execution of your new plans?
91. Do you like to travel?
92. Do you take vacations?
93. What is your favorite vacation destination?
94. Have you traveled to Europe, Africa, or Asia?
95. Do you speak any foreign languages?
96. What do you think about the immigration issue in America?
97. Do you celebrate holidays in a big way or do they just come and go?
98. Do you need an alarm clock to wake up?
99. What is your morning ritual?
100. What is your educational background?
101. How important is education to you?
102. Did you like school?
103. Did you get good grades?
104. Do you have any health challenges?
105. Do you take medication? (If yes) For what and for how long?
106. Do you follow your doctor's advice?
107. What are you doing to correct this health challenge?
108. Are you willing to make sacrifices to have no health challenges?
109. Are you a healthy eater?
110. Do you cook?
111. Do you like ice cream?
112. What are your favorite foods?
113. What is your favorite restaurant?
114. How often do you eat out?
115. Do you exercise?
116. Are you athletic?

117. What is your favorite sport?

118. What is your favorite team?

119. Do you get annual checkups?

120. Have you had a prostate exam or a mammogram?

121. Are you a workaholic?

122. Do you stress easily?

123. Do you care what other people say about you?

124. How do you think other people view you?

125. Do you gossip?

126. Do you tell the truth no matter what, even if it hurts someone's feelings?

127. Are there any secrets that you will carry to your grave?

128. Have you been to jail?

129. Do you think that incarceration is the answer to the ills of our society?

130. What ill of our society would you choose to eliminate?

131. What do you think is causing us the most trouble as Americans today?

132. Do you vote?

133. Are you Republican, Democrat, or Independent, and why?

134. Is there any cause that you wholeheartedly support?

135. Do you believe we have a responsibility to the planet?

136. Do you like to go out?

137. Do you drink?

138. (If yes) Is drinking a problem for you?

139. Do you do drugs?

140. Do you smoke?

141. What are your favorite places to go for fun?

142. What do you consider fun?
143. How do you relax?
144. How do you feel about attending formals?
145. Do you own a tuxedo or a gown?
146. Do you have a dress suit?
147. What entertainment genre most affects our society?
148. What do you consider beautiful?
149. Is your culture important to you?
150. What do you do to celebrate your culture?
151. Do you drive? (In New York City, I've met more people who don't drive, especially men, than I've encountered anywhere else.)
152. Do you have a car?
153. Do you own a home?
154. Do you have good credit?
155. Is it important to date a person of equal earnings?
156. Have you ever filed for bankruptcy?
157. What are your financial goals for yourself?
158. Do you want to retire wealthy?
159. Do you live for the moment or from check to check?
160. Do you save money?
161. What do you spend the most money on?
162. What is your largest monthly expense?
163. Do you think there is such a thing as being too rich?
164. What tempts you the most?
165. Are there any obstacles that may prohibit you from reaching your goals?
166. If you could change one thing in your life, what would it be?
167. What was your most embarrassing moment?
168. What is your most important life's achievement?

169. Do you like to read?

170. What is your favorite book?

171. What is your most memorable moment?

172. What was your most frightening moment?

173. Is it important for others to know you are successful?

174. Do you feel you have to keep up with the Joneses?

175. Are you forgiving?

176. Do you have terms for forgiveness?

177. Do you love unconditionally?

178. Do you leave room for others to make mistakes?

179. Is it easy for you to apologize?

180. Is it easy for you to accept apologies?

181. Do you forgive and forget?

182. What is your favorite movie?

183. Who is your favorite movie star?

184. What is your favorite song?

185. Who is your favorite artist?

186. What is on your CD player at home right now?

187. Where do you see yourself settling down: city, suburbs, or a rural town?

188. What season do you enjoy the most?

189. How are you most misunderstood?

190. Are you competitive?

191. If you could address an audience of 10,000 people tomorrow, what topic would you choose?

192. Who is the role model in your life?

193. Do you hang out a lot with your friends?

194. What do you and your friends like to do most?

195. Do you have a standing date or an annual jaunt with friends?

196. What do you never leave the house without?
197. In whom do you confide?
198. To whom are you accountable?
199. If you could let go of one thing in your life, what would it be?
200. If you were a pastor, what sermon would you preach?

. . . And the answers to these questions—and others—will make you free, keep you negative, and give you the insight you need *before* you let them touch you. As I always say: Before you swap spit, swap information. This is how you can stay safe. Information is power. Do *not* perish for lack of knowledge. *Ask!*

How to Stay Well

In addition to being covered by the Blood of Jesus, which allowed me to avoid becoming infected with the virus after multiple exposures, I am convinced my good health is due to the holistic lifestyle that I have practiced since my late teens. As a result, my immune system is rock solid.

Now, as Dr. LaJoyce Brookshire, naturopathic doctor, master herbalist, and doctor of naturopathic ministry, I'd like to share some ways that you too can bolster your immune health.

• Drink half your body weight in ounces of high-quality filtered or spring water daily (i.e., if you weigh one hundred and fifty pounds, then you should drink seventy-five ounces). Remember, if you feel thirsty, then dehydration has already set in. If you are able to make only one health change in your life, make it this one.

Water has been my primary beverage for more than twenty years. I always add lemon to my water in restaurants, because lemon kills many bacteria that may be in the water by making the water acidic, while becoming alkaline ash in the stomach. I also like to cut up fresh fruit, fill the bottom of a pitcher with berries, watermelon, or mango, and pour water over the fruit. I let the container sit in the refrigerator overnight, and in the morning I have real fruit water. Nothing added, and the water totally takes on the flavor of the fruit. This is the real Fruit2O.

Additionally, I drink most of my water laced with chlorophyll because it mimics red blood cells and aids in strengthening them. I like the chlorophyll made by Nature's Sunshine, which has a spearmint flavor, making it more palatable as a primary beverage. I pour in the chlorophyll concentrate until the water becomes dark green. Yes, I carry bottles of green water—it's a great conversation piece.

A must read:

Your Body's Many Cries for Water: You're Not Sick, You're Thirsty by Fereydoon Batmanghelidj, M.D.

- Every day, make a superfood green drink loaded with chlorophyll, spirulina, wheatgrass, barley, blue-green algae, and chlorella. I recommend any superfood like Vita-Mineral Greens, Barlean's Green, or Kyo-Green, and I put it in a smoothie with frozen fruit and Green Goodness juice by Bolthouse Farms.

I also recommend SuperGreens which is loaded with sixty-seven grasses and leaves to restore alkalinity to the body. This product helps diabetics restore insulin levels. You can order it at www.innerlightfoundation.org.

A must read:

The pH Miracle by Dr. Robert O. Young and Shelley Redford Young

• Take a liquid multivitamin daily.

I am an advocate of liquids, powders, and chewables, instead of pills, because they are bioavailable for immediate use in the body. I recommend E3Live, the world's first and only fresh-frozen live Aphanizomenon flos-aquae (AFA). It contains more chlorophyll than wheatgrass; 60 percent high-quality protein; all B vitamins including B12; omega-3 and omega-6; digestive enzymes; and anti-aging nutrients. E3Live comes frozen to your door via FedEx. Try it for yourself: 888-800-7070 or www.e3live.com.

• The more white bread, the sooner you're dead!

Eliminate the nasty whites—bread, pasta, rice, and sugar. These are devitalized foods that tear down your immune system. Never eat white bread; choose multigrain breads instead. Never use margarine or butter spreads; choose *real* butter always. Do not consume any aspartame products (Equal, Sweet 'n Low); these are all poisons and the primary culprits behind new diseases with fancy names like fibromyalgia.

Additionally, stay away from foods that God did not grow in the garden. Man is not smart enough to *make* food! Avoid hybrid foods like pluots and iceberg lettuce (that is acid and does your body more harm than good).

The public has been tricked by propaganda and slick advertising to believe that products like I Can't Believe It's Not Butter and other spreads are healthy choices. Don't believe it's butter—because it's not! Those spreads don't even melt right away when you put them in boiling water. Enough said.

A must read:
Back to Eden by Jethro Kloss
A must subscribe:
www.mercola.com

- Eat mainly green, leafy, and raw vegetables.

Your diet should consist of 60 percent raw foods. To accomplish this, I begin with a full plate of salad as if it were going to be my meal, then I put my hot food on top of the salad. I get the hot/cold and crunchy/soft combo— which I love—with every bite. Remember, my nickname was Rabbit.

This will also help you to establish alkalinity in the body. Acid in the body is the origin of most diseases. Buy saliva pH strips in the health food store to test yourself regularly.

A must read:
Alkalize or Die by Theodore A. Brody

- Eat at least five fruits a day.

I eat my fruits for breakfast, and this way I know I have eaten them all. Be careful not to combine fruits with other foods, as they putrefy in the stomach, making digestion difficult. Fruits should be eaten alone, at least two hours after or before eating other foods. Do not combine melons with other fruits. Eat them alone.

I like to cut up my fruits and freeze them so that they are readily available for making a smoothie instead of using ice. I also love to puree fruits like strawberries or pears and use them as ice cubes in homemade lemonade or juices.

A must read:
Fit for Life by Harvey Diamond
A must subscribe:
www.notmilk.com

• Cut down on the contaminants you put in your body.

The world today is filled with many toxins that overload our adrenal systems and our organs. It is important to remove the things that can make us sick. As we continue to be bombarded with known carcinogens in our products—like sodium lauryl sulfate in some soap products, fluoride in toothpaste and in most drinking water, and aspartame in many store-bought foods—we need to restore our cells so that they can fight these toxins.

I use a product called Natural Cellular Defense. It is a zeolite, which is liquid volcanic ash. It is an oral chelation product that breaks down heavy metals and toxins, making them small enough to leave your body. Natural Cellular Defense can also be used topically on warts or tumors; it shrank a cyst on my shoulder in two weeks. I consider this a wonder product because it works in a very short time on myriad issues. There have been reports on Natural Cellular Defense shrinking cancerous tumors as well as reversing autism.

Order at 866-699-2467 or www.mywaiora.com.

• Eliminate beef and pork from your diet.

These foods take too long to digest and make your elimination system work overtime. You will lose that "sluggish" feeling after eating if you eliminate these foods.

• Buy organic or local farm-fresh foods, as a rule.

When in season, local fresh is an excellent choice. Yes, organic foods are more expensive, but I say you can pay now or pay later. The old adage "You Are What You Eat" is true. You are not only what you eat, but also what you digest and what you eliminate. You should have a bowel movement after every meal for optimum colon health. Death really does begin in the colon. To aid in digestion, try three to four digestive enzymes before each meal. I like DGL by Enzymatic Therapy.

• Go to bed!

I have been a sleepyhead since I could remember, but I rise very early. I've learned that this pattern keeps our body clocks in sync with nature. We are designed to rise and retire with the sun. Your body can repair itself *only* when you are sleeping during the night. It has to do with the restorative properties of the moon. Make a point of retiring by 10 P.M. and creating a ritual for yourself. I like to bathe; relax by reading, journaling, or changing channels; turn off the lights and the TV; and then sleep. My internal clock awakens me during the four o'clock hour. When I wake up, I get up.

- Get exercise.

I like to power-walk and attend ballet, African, and jazz dance classes. When I can't go outside, I get some exercise by parking in the farthest corner of a parking lot and walking to do errands. I take stairs whenever I can, and I clean my own house.

- Eliminate stress.

Take a look at the things in your life that may stress you. In many cases it may be your job, but saying "good morning" at the nine-to-five will be easier if you have a Plan B—an avocation that you love or a business plan in the wings that will one day set you free from the daily grind. If it is a toxic relationship, seek counseling with that person. If the person means you well, they will honor your request. Upon making such a suggestion, you will uncover the truth.

I like to take my stresses to the bathtub, and as I wash away the day, I consider all that has troubled me. When I release the drain, I allow all I've washed off to leave me, by going down the drain.

- De-stress!

For those stresses that sneak up on me when I'm not near my tub, I keep a bottle of the holistic product Bach Rescue Remedy in my purse and administer five drops under the tongue. This is a bottled flower essence designed to capture the calm of just having received flowers. It works!

- Fight Father Time.

Let's face it, aging begins at birth. In order to keep the

three million cells you create every day well, you need a super antioxidant. I love the product called AgelessXtra by Univera LifeSciences. It comes in two-ounce bottles to take with you, and not only can it knock the edge off your hunger, it is a whole food and can help you to halt the aging process by making repairs at the cellular level. I love it! Visit us.univera.com.

HOLISTIC HEALTH CARE PROVIDERS

If you are having trouble following a regimen to improve your health, seek out a holistic health care practitioner to help get you on track. Here are a few holistic health care practitioners whom I know to be fabulous, providing their patients and clients with alternative modalities of treatment by practicing wellness:

Dr. Frederick Burton, M.D. and Alternative Therapy
Doctor
Burton Wellness & Injury Center
1455 City Line Ave.
Wynnewood, PA 19096
610-649-4325
-or-
321 East Emmaus Ave.
Allentown, PA 18103
610-791-2453
www.burtonwellnesscenter.com

Robinson Wellness Center
Dr. Fadairo Afolabi—Chiropractic Physician
Dr. Abdel Salaam—M.D., Colon Therapist
Dr. LaJoyce Brookshire—Naturopathic Doctor,
    Master Herbalist
Cleta McCloud—Licensed Clinical Social Worker
Chief Afolabi—Master Herbalist
Omilade—Certified Massage Therapist
304 Park Ave.
East Orange, NJ 07017
973-678-7575
www.RobinsonWellnessCenter.com

SCARED STRAIGHT: What You Don't Know
    About HIV *Can* Kill You
An HIV Educational Program developed for ages
    eleven to adult
Presented by:
Dr. Fadairo Afolabi and Dr. LaJoyce Brookshire
Robinson Wellness Center
973-678-7575

Dr. William Holder, M.D.
Center for Preventive Medicine
285 N. Beverwyck Road
Parsippany, NJ 07054
973-678-7575

Dr. Nora Presley, Integrative M.D.
(Specializing in Complementary and Alternative
  Medicine)
The Cinderella Foundation
65 W. 96th St.
New York, NY 10025
212-865-3930

Queen Afua
Heal Thyself Natural Living Center
106 Kingston Ave.
Brooklyn, NY 11213
718-221-HEAL
www.QueenAfuaOnline.com

Dr. Newvelvet Washington
Dr. Martina Washington
New Life Wellness Center
426 8th Street S.E., 2nd floor
Washington, DC 20003
202-544-9595
www.NewLifeWellnessCenter.com

Karyn Calabrese
Karyn's Inner Beauty Center
1901 North Halsted St.
Chicago, IL 60614
312-255-1590
www.KarynRaw.com

Dr. Kenneth Ackles, Sr., D.C., Chiropractic Physician
3231 N. Meridian St., Suite 502
Indianapolis, IN 46208
317-926-4623
KenAckles@sbcglobal.net

Stream of Life Holistic Health & Colonic Center
(specializing in nutritional consultations, reflexology,
fasting classes; carries a complete selection of
Nature's Sunshine products)
754 E. 82nd St.
Chicago, IL 60619
773-994-6323
streamoflife@sbcglobal.net

Dr. Marcia B. Williams, Naturopathic Doctor
(specializing in dark field microscopy, nutritional
consultations, autonomic response testing, and
advanced Jaffe-Mellor Technique)
Greater Atlanta Area
404-931-9903
MW4health@yahoo.com

Dr. Sebi
2807 La Cienega Ave.
Los Angeles, CA 90034
310-838-2490

Russell Harrison, Master Herbalist
(specializes in detoxification, all cancers, and immune
   boosters through wild-crafted organic herbs
   handmade by Russell)
Russell Herbal Company
7501 Crenshaw Blvd.
Los Angeles, CA 90045
323-751-1461
www.russellherbal.com

Dr. Juneau K. Robbins
Cultural Chiropractic, P.A.
617 Harry Davis Ln.
Minneapolis, MN 55411
612-819-9634
Drjuneaurobbins@aol.com

Dr. Desvill James
Dr. Razak Bologun
Dr. Lawson Homiard
Bazile Spine Center
5600 South Willow, Suite 115
Houston, TX 77035
713-726-9111

Dr. Judith L. Hatch, Doctor of Chiropractic
Holistic Healthcare in Albany
1144 Dawson Rd.
Albany, GA 31707
229-888-1005
judithhatch@yahoo.com

Dr. Corrine Morgan
Morgan Chiropractic Center Services
1019 Christian St.
Philadelphia, PA 19147
215-922-4782
Cmorgan@chiropractic.com

Dr. Romanuel Washington, Jr.
Dr. Madeline Washington
Chiropractic Arts & Science Clinic
3300 Crawford St.
Houston, TX 77004
713-522-3878
drmaddydc@yahoo.com

Dr. Herman J. Glass II
Glass Chiropractic Health Plaza
17301 W. Eight Mile Rd.
Detroit, MI 48235
313-533-BACK (2225)
drglassii@sbcglobal.net

Dr. Cal Whitworth
Mattapan Chiropractic & Rehab
1537 Blue Hill Ave.
Mattapan, MA 02126
617-298-1370

Dr. Rashida Cohen, Chiropractic Physician
Advantage Rehabilitation & Wellness Center
1145 19th St. N.W., Suite 308
Washington, DC 20036
202-835-BACK (2225)
www.caringchiropractor.com

WHERE TO GET HELP

**National Black Leadership Commission on AIDS,
    Inc. (BLCA)**
105 E. 22nd St.
New York, NY 10010
212-614-0023
800-992-6531
www.nblca.org

Direct Service Providers
The Balm in Gilead
New York, NY
www.balmingilead.org

Black AIDS Institute
Los Angeles, CA
www.blackaids.org

Community Health Outreach Workers
Detroit, MI
www.chowlinks.org

Education, Training & Research
Scotts Valley, CA
www.etr.org

Harm Reduction Coalition
New York, NY
www.harmreduction.org

Jackson State University
Jackson, MS
www.jsums.edu

Metropolitan Interdenominational Church
Nashville, TN
www.metropolitanfrc.com

National AIDS Education Services for Minorities
Atlanta, GA
www.naesmonline.org

National Black Alcoholism & Addictions Council
Orlando, FL
www.nbacinc.org

National Minority AIDS Council
Washington, DC
www.nmac.org

National Youth Advocacy Coalition
Washington, DC
www.nyacyouth.org

Technical Assistance Providers

Aegis (AIDS Education Global Information System)
www.aegis.com

American Red Cross
Washington, DC
www.redcross.org

The Ark of Refuge, Inc.
San Francisco, CA
www.arkofrefuge.org

The Body: The Complete HIV/AIDS Resource
New York, NY
www.thebody.com/aac/aacpage.html

CDC National Prevention Information Network
Rockville, MD
www.cdcnpin.org

Centers for Disease Control and Prevention
Atlanta, GA
www.cdc.gov

Computerized AIDS Ministries
New York, NY
www.gbgm-umc.org/cam/

The Elizabeth Glaser Pediatric AIDS Foundation
Washington, DC
www.pedaids.org

The Family Center
New York, NY
www.thefamilycenter.org

Global Health Council
Washington, DC
www.globalhealth.org

Health Power
Brooklyn, NY
www.healthpoweronline.com

The Henry J. Kaiser Family Foundation
Menlo Park, CA
www.kff.org

HIV/AIDS Manual for Faith Communities—
    National Coalition of Pastors' Spouses
Memphis, TN
www.pastorsspouses.com

HIV InSite
San Francisco, CA
www.hivinsite.ucsf.edu/InSite

HIVPositive.com
www.hivpositive.com

National Association of People with AIDS
Silver Spring, MD
www.napwa.org

The National Institutes of Health
Bethesda, MD
www.nih.gov

Project Inform
San Francisco, CA
www.projinf.org

SisterLove, Inc.
Atlanta, GA
www.sisterlove.org

Treatment Action Group
New York, NY
www.aidsinfonyc.org/tag/index.html

UNAIDS
Geneva, Switzerland
www.unaids.org

U.S. Department of Health and Human Services
Washington, DC
www.hhs.gov

U.S. Department of Health and Human Services
     Health Resources and Services Administration
Rockville, MD
www.hab.hrsa.gov

Research Sites

American Foundation for AIDS Research
New York, NY
www.amfar.org

Gay Men's Health Crisis
New York, NY
www.gmhc.org

Resources

The Body
Religion & HIV/AIDS Resources
New York, NY
www.thebody.com/religion.html

Housing Works
Brooklyn, NY
www.housingworks.org

Lambda Legal Defense and Education Fund
New York, NY
www.lambdalegal.org

National Catholic AIDS Network
Chicago, IL
www.ncan.org

New York AIDS Coalition
New York, NY
www.nyaidscoalition.org

Project Inform Women's Treatment Issues Site
San Francisco, CA
www.projectinform.org/ww/ww_index.html

Online Newsletters

News Rx
Atlanta, GA
www.newsfile.com/la.html

Poz Magazine
New York, NY
www.POZ.com